Reagan Electionomics

Reagan Electionomics
How Reagan Ambushed the
Pollsters

Green Hill Publishers
Ottawa, Illinois

Copies of this book may be purchased from the distributor for $14.95. All inquiries and catalogue requests should be addressed to Green Hill Publishers, P. O. Box 738, Ottawa, Ill. 61350. (815) 434-7905.

Published by Green Hill Publishers, Ottawa, Illinois.

To the dedicated men and women who prepared the way for Ronald Reagan's election as president of the United States

Contents

Tables

Foreword

Why the Reagan Victory?

THE CONSERVATIVE tide that swept over the nation in November of 1980 came as a surprise to many commentators and analysts of popular opinion.

The major reason for the astonishment was the contrast between the outcome and the expectation of the pollsters. Most opinion surveys had depicted a seesaw election; one showed President Carter pulling ahead toward the end; virtually none foretold the landslide that was in the making.

The election outcome was also in vivid conflict with long-term poll surveys suggesting the American people, despite a generalized conservatism in their attitudes, are firmly liberal on specific policy questions. This view has been supported by reference to poll surveys showing popular backing for government medical care, old-age assistance, aid to the needy, and other specific measures to help the impoverished.

A lot of confusion on this score is cleared up in the chapters that follow. They were written at different times over the past decade by Donald J. Devine, who is now the director of the U.S. Office of Personnel Management in the Reagan administration. Before joining the government, he was professor of political science at the University of Maryland. In this book, Devine examines the premise that Americans are basically liberal, finds it to be false, and demonstrates why Ronald Reagan enjoyed such a tremendous victory at the polls in 1980.

In examining the longstanding academic thesis that the American people are favorably oriented toward government welfare measures, Devine finds that a large part of the problem is the way the pollsters approach their subjects. If people are asked whether they favor some noble-sounding objective or program of social uplift as a general proposition, they are likely to answer in the affirmative. Surveys purporting to show strong support for welfare-state objectives tend to be of this nature; for example: "Do you agree or disagree that government ought to help people get doctors and hospital care at low cost?"

On the other hand, if people are asked to suggest problem areas or policy initiatives on an open-ended basis, without guidance from the poll-taker, they tend to respond differently—naming issues and problems other than those dictated by welfare-state ideology. And if they are asked to match up benefits with costs, or choose among methods of obtaining desirable goals in addition to central government action, the results are more different still. From all of which it would appear that spontaneous support for national welfarism is relatively weak.

Over against these findings about the supposed benefits of government there has been a growing body of data in recent years suggesting an increased awareness of costs: concern about taxes, overregulation, too much spending, and the like have surfaced in surveys that do weigh the options, and have also tended to surface in the polling place. Analysts who put such findings together with the weakness of the data allegedly revealing enthusiasm for the welfare state would not have been perplexed by the 1980 election.

What has apparently happened in many opinion surveys, and the interpretations placed on them, is that the poll-takers or interpreters have tended to load their own values into the process, cuing responses from the public in the way in which the questions were asked and options posed (or not posed). In this respect, much poll-taking has been an exercise in self-fulfilling prophecy, rather than objective inquiry into the state of public attitudes.

The point emerges clearly from the researches of Dr. Devine. On his evidence, there is nothing very surprising about such recent developments as the tax revolt, the general shift of the nation toward conservatism, or the Reagan victory in 1980. The pollsters were prevented from seeing the landslide that was coming because their methods wouldn't let them see it.

In a similar vein, this book makes clear to those who hold the future course of the Republican party in their hands that the Reagan revolution can be the dominant force in American politics for decades to come if they will only recognize the reasons why they won in 1980, and act to solidify the conservative direction of government in the years to come.

M. STANTON EVANS

Acknowledgments

I WOULD like to thank *Human Events,* and its editors, Thomas S. Winter and Alan Ryskind, for permission to reprint several articles that were printed by them at the time. I would also like to thank M. Stanton Evans, chairman of the American Conservative Union's Educational and Research Institute, for permission to reprint one chapter, and especially for writing the Foreword. And I would like to thank the editors of the political science journal *Polity* for permission to reprint another chapter. The facts used in this book are not footnoted; but references are available in the original manuscripts. The scholarly reader is directed to those sources. Of course, I absolve all parties from the sins of the book.

Introduction

THE THESIS of this book is that the Reagan revolution occurred because of three underlying realities: American politics is dynamic and allows for change; the American people were basically predisposed toward conservative values; and there was a catalyst conservative movement that had prepared for the opportunity. I first became associated with this conservative enterprise through Young Americans for Freedom in 1960. I have been a strategist of sorts for that enterprise, also through the American Conservative Union, ever since. During that time I probably have been associated with more losing elections than any other man in history. But I have been doing better lately.

Following a particularly disastrous defeat—the hammer-blow congressional defeat in 1962, as a result of President Kennedy's well-timed action on the Cuban missile crisis—I wrote a piece telling my fellow conservatives to prepare for a twenty-year organizational effort. It was apparent that we did not have the trained political or philosophical personnel, that the mass-media oligarchy would not allow us access to reach the people, and that we could not raise money from a corporate America which feared conservatism would place businesses at the mercy of the market.

Young Americans for Freedom and the American Conservative Union first began work on the personnel problem. They focused their efforts on leadership training, as they were taught by Frank Meyer. Richard Viguerie (an early executive director of YAF) then came along with an idea called direct mail. This mechanism allowed conservatives to outflank both the mass media (so we could present our message directly to individuals) and corporate America (so we could obtain contributions directly from the grass roots).

The first major success was in 1964, in spite of a massive general-election defeat. Even at the time, few of the leaders emphasized the general election, or thought it could be won. At a meeting of the board of directors of Young Americans for Freedom in the early summer of 1964, before the nomination, a poll was taken asking whether Barry Goldwater would win the general election. The board was unanimous in voting that he would not. The point of the 1964 campaign was that, for the first time, conservatives gained essential control over the Republican party. And it provided an opportunity to expand the movement many hundredfold. The millions of individuals who were recruited as activists during that campaign gave conservatives the raw material for all of their activities and campaigns between 1964 and 1968, and beyond.

Most conservatives supported Richard Nixon in the 1968 campaign. They soon became disenchanted, however. So they began organizing again for control of the Republican party. They were successful enough that, even though President Nixon controlled the 1972 convention, conservatives won the major battle that year, on rules. This was in spite of the fact that the conservative leaders were directly warned by John Erlichman not do so, and were threatened with ostracism from the Republican party if we did. Against the wishes of the White House staff, conservative activists persisted and won by two-to-one margins in the committees and on the floor. One of the participants in the floor fight was the governor of California, Ronald Reagan.

Between 1972 and 1976 I served on the Republican "Rule 29" Committee, which was formed so that our party could "catch up" with the McGovernite reforms in the Democratic party. Although the committee was purposely stacked against the conservatives, we prevailed on the essential items in the final report, at the National Committee, and finally at the National Convention. By 1976, conservatives had already united behind Ronald Reagan for president. And we very nearly won the nomination from a sitting president. This book begins at that point.

The reader is entitled to know, if it is not obvious already, that I was far from a disinterested observer of the 1980 election. In 1976 I was Maryland state chairman for Ronald Reagan's presidential campaign, and was chief political adviser on convention rules (the eminent Roger Alan Moore was and is chief legal adviser on rules). In 1980 I was deputy director of political planning and analysis, political leader on rules again, regional political director, and Maryland state chairman for the man who became president. In spite of this close association, I believe the analysis, as opposed to the opinion, in this book is objective.

The chapters in this book, except the last two, were written well before the 1980 election. They truly are products of both politics and political science—that is, they use political science tools to understand reality, to predict it, to help shape a rational strategy to deal with it, and to win elections with it.

Following the election, I was named by the president to be transition team leader for the agencies of government that deal with civil-service personnel matters. A few months later I was named director of the U.S. Office of Personnel Management. In that role I have been able to assist the president in achieving his goals. Since entering office, the Reagan administration has been able to reduce nondefense government employment by 113,000 (as of spring 1983). And we have been able to do it through the most humane and efficient means, at a sustained rate greater than at any other time since World War II. I have been able to save billions in employee disability retirement, the federal employees' health insurance program (and was able to limit abortions for 80 percent of covered employees), in early government retirements, and under the special pay rate program.

In March 1983 the president approved our proposals for a program called Fulfilling the Civil Service Reform Ideal in the Centennial Year. It is the most ambitious step in reforming the civil service in years. Its purpose is to remove disincentives to making government work efficiently. First, it makes performance the central part of government personnel management: extending the concept of pay-for-performance to 1.4 million members of the white-collar workforce, and running layoffs more on the basis of performance than of seniority.

Second, we propose a major reform of the federal employees' retirement system, to grab hold of its escalating costs, and to build a rational compensation package. Between 1960 and 1981, government outlays for the Civil Service Retirement System increased by 2,300 percent, compared to 1,200 percent for social security. There was an unfunded liability of half a trillion dollars—half again of the whole national debt. Our proposal would move the normal retirement age from fifty-five to sixty-five, put a limit on cost-of-living adjustments, increase employee contributions to make them mutually supported by government and employees, and make the benefit formula comparable to those in the private sector.

Third, we would create a voucher system within our employees' health-benefit program. This would not only reduce the cost of administering the program, but also result in lower premiums for our employees through market competition.

Personnel expenses represent over 15 percent of total government expenditures. That is about $100 billion per year. An important part of the president's pledge to bring government under control is to bring the size, expense, and work processes of the government under control.

As director of the U.S. government's civil service, I have had an opportunity to participate in a practical way to correct what in the past I have only been able to teach. Over the years, through books, lectures and speeches, political activity, and now government, I have been privileged to be part of the movement to restore America's greatness. In this, we have all been sustained by the support given by the men and women who prepared the way for Ronald Reagan's election as president. For this reason, this book is dedicated to them.

Part I

The People

Chapter 1

The Answer Depends on the Question*

HOW DO you find out what people think about politics? Simple; you ask them questions. Yet, this is not an obvious process. One must know what questions to ask and what form the question should take. Here we will take a close look at three forms:
1. the assertion question, where respondents are asked to agree or disagree;
2. the dichotomous question, which poses two alternative choices; and
3. the multiple-choice question, which presents several alternatives.

Why focus on form? Because in several studies I have made of the more reliable public opinion polls taken since the beginning of scientific polling in 1935, the influence of the number and type of response categories has proven to be of central importance in describing public opinion. Clearly, if the descriptions are invalid, then the explanatory role of public opinion research is subject to question.

An interesting case study can be found in the early days of scientific polling. George Gallup's early descriptions of opinion in his newspaper columns, and Elmo Roper's in *Fortune* magazine, were very different. These journalistic reports are interesting because they are the major sources of

---

* Adapted from an article appearing in *Polity*, spring 1980. It appears here because before we can understand the genesis of the Reagan revolution, we must explain why it appears to defy conventional wisdom about the supposedly liberal nature of the American electorate. Conventional wisdom, it turns out, is strongly influenced by the media and other communications, which are affected by polling methods that tend to produce distorted results. This article explains why. Reprinted with permission.

the early years of public opinion polls. The telling fact is that the interpretations of the results contradicted each other for the major issues of the day. Gallup found large majorities agreeing to questions favorable to the New Deal, and concluded that Americans were demanding solutions by the national government. By contrast, Roper found less than majority support for the New Deal solutions because pluralities of Americans preferred private, business, or local government means to intercession by the national government in public policy terms.

What caused this difference? They both used the same survey methodology, and neither used biased questions to any great extent. The difference was that, on questions of policy, Gallup tended to use assertion questions, and Roper generally relied upon open-ended or multiple-choice questions.

In the language of the political scientist, assertion questions contain an affirmative "response set" bias: that is, no variation in the response is possible—it's either yes or no. There is no room for subtlety; so people tend to say yes to positively worded questions. But there is another less well known but more serious inherent bias, regardless of whether the question is worded affirmatively or negatively: if a question contains two or more ideas, one positive or negative symbol can determine the answer, even if the investigator is interested in one of the other ideas.

Consequently, assertion-type questions tend to obtain majority support because the respondent frequently has to agree when a symbol he favors is linked to a means he does not favor. For example, if asked whether the government should take a certain action to achieve prosperity or eliminate poverty, he finds it difficult to disagree with the means without rejecting the symbolic goal of prosperity for all. Therefore, most respondents tend to support whatever means are presented, as long as they are linked with approved goals.

The answers change fundamentally when questions contrast two alternatives. Opinions tend to divide more equally. Still, by definition, when only two choices are given, one alternative must receive a majority. This is a critical feature for democracy, which acts on the basis of majority rule. Majoritarian democracy is always searching for dichotomies—in referendums, in two-party elections, and in poll questions. The reason is clear: two choices simplify opinion, and one choice can obtain a majority.

Pluralists, like Roper (at least when he polled for *Fortune*), tend to find beliefs more complex—both in themselves and in their effect upon public policy. They see a range of values and opinions, extending along a continuum from the pole of support through a neutral zone in the middle to the pole of opposition, rather than majorities and minorities. This perspective tends to emphasize the middle of the range, although opinion is expected to be spread throughout the range of possible beliefs—that is, to be plural.

The proper way of reflecting the complexity of this range is through open-ended questions, which allow each person to give his own reply. The multiple-choice form also tends to show the desired plurality because opinions divide among the various options presented, and no one choice easily obtains a majority.

Describing American Public Opinion

A look at the major public opinion studies published in the United States shows how each of these types of questions has influenced the description of American public opinion. A picture of the country as favoring liberal welfare-state policies is most often found in the first and largest category, wherein selective assertion-type questions are used. Invariably, such surveys show that the liberal policies favored by the overwhelming proportion of poll-takers have been supported by a "majority," by "an overwhelming majority," or by a "consensus" of Americans.

A variation on this type utilizes both an ideological and a policy dimension, in which it is found that although a large majority of Americans is opposed to welfare programs of the national government at the ideological level, when it comes to specific programs (federal aid to education, federally financed medical care, or federal welfare), a majority supports these liberal policies. But despite the fact that questions posing alternatives are used for some parts of such studies, the major questions used to measure opinion on public policy invariably rely on the same simple assertion form. As a result, the conclusions are the same— namely, that on policy Americans are overwhelmingly liberal even if they are conservative with respect to more basic values.

In the second category, where poll questions pose dichotomous policy alternatives, the conclusions tend to be less clear as to whether the people are liberal on policy. In a study done during the Truman era, one political scientist found that "although there is much criticism of the 'welfare state,' the polls . . . indicated it is being gradually accepted." Likewise, a decade later, two other researchers found "the existence of a generally favorable public disposition toward federal aid to education, but little deep interest" and several "divisions" among the public on the type of aid desired. Interestingly, in an analysis of the same subject several years later, another political scientist found majority support for federal aid to education in 1956 and 1960 when questions without alternatives were used but only minority support in 1964 when a question posing alternatives was used.

The difference in interpretation when different question forms are used is dramatically shown in the case of federal aid to education. Since the 1930s, polls have found that large majorities have agreed with questions that asked in general terms if people supported federal aid to education. As shown in the first column of Table 1, support continued into the 1950s and 1960s. Yet, in 1964 and 1968, when the choice was of having the government in Washington help provide education or having it handled only by state and local governments, more people chose not to have national government help. The fact that both types of questions were asked at approximately the same time in 1964 suggests that the form of the question was critical.

Table 1
Public Opinion on Federal Aid to Education

	Assertion-Type Question	Alternative Question		
	Support Federal Aid	National Help	Don't Know	State-Local Only
SRC 1956	67%	—	—	—
AIPO 1960	65	—	—	—
SRC 1960	53	—	—	—
AIPO 1964	62	—	—	—
SRC 1964	—	31	22	47
SRC 1968	—	28	24	48

SOURCE: SRC from ICPR; AIPO release dated 2/19/60; and Lloyd A. Free and Hadley Cantril, *The Political Beliefs of Americans* (New Brunswick, N.J.: Rutgers University Press, 1967), p. 189.

The same sort of problem exists when considering support for federal financing of health care generally and of health care only for the aged. A study done in 1972 did include a look at questions providing alternatives, but it included a summary table which mixed questions that posed alternatives with questions that did not (Table 2). The impression given by this table is that support has changed over time. The author concluded that "most expressions of government participation in health-care financing were so strong that it is legitimate to view the data as strong evidence of popular majority support." Yet all of the cases of majority support, except one, were based on question forms that did not offer an alternative. The only instance showing majority support involved medicare for the aged, and this question was asked before debate on the issue began. Two months later, support dropped below a majority—although there was still plurality support. In the area of comprehensive health insurance, the national government alternative was not even supported by a plurality in three of the four years for which questions posing alternatives are available.

Table 2
Public Opinion on Government Medical Insurance

	Range of Percent Supporting
1936	79
1937	80
1938	81
1942	74–78
1943	44–58
1945	52–68
1949	33–45
1956	54–68
1960	60–75
1962	40–48
1964	50–64
1968	62

SOURCE: Mark V. Nadel, "Public Policy and Public Opinion," in *American Democracy: Theory and Reality,* ed. Robert Weissberg and Mark V. Nadel (New York: Wiley, 1972), p. 533.

The situation is similar for welfare policy. When asked simple assertion questions, large majorities have said that "the government should provide for all people who have no means of obtaining a living." But when they are given the choice of whether the national government or the state-local government should handle the problem, Table 3 shows that more have preferred the latter. The reason most other descriptions of welfare opinion come to a different conclusion is quite simply that they do not consider this option.

Table 3
Public Opinion on Welfare

	AIPO[1] 1936	FOR[2] 1937	AIPO[3] 1939	AIPO[4] 1961
Federal	45%	35%	36%	29%
State-local	55	46	64	55
Combination	—	6	—	—
None	—	3	—	—
Don't know	—	10	—	16[5]

[1] Actual question: Should the responsibility of caring for all persons be returned now to the state and local governments? (assertion).

[2] Actual question: Which kind of government—federal, state, or local—do you feel should take care of relief?

[3] Actual question: Do you think unemployment relief should be handled by the federal government or by state and local governments?

[4] Actual question: At present most of the regulations dealing with persons on relief come from the state government or Washington. Would you like to have this policy continued or would you give local communities more say as to which persons should get relief and how much?

[5] SOURCE: Hadley Cantril with Mildred Strunk, *Public Opinion, 1935-1946* (Princeton, N.J.: Princeton University Press, 1951), pp. 893-96, nos. 3, 29, 35; and AIPO release dated 8/11/61.

The third category consists of questions that pose several alternatives, or even open-ended questions, in a more pluralistic manner. Not surprisingly, this approach rarely shows clear majority support for any alternative. In the case of the health-care financing survey data mentioned earlier, another political scientist who looked at the same material concluded, after looking at all the alternatives, that "the data available on the health insurance issues neither affirm nor deny public support for the principle of social insurance." Table 4 shows the data from one of the few studies using the pluralist mode of question systematically through a range of policies. These data show that the welfare-state solution of using the national government has far less support than the use of individual-family-private, or the local-state government alternatives. Indeed, at most, 26 percent chose the national solution.

Table 4
Pluralist Public Opinion on Issues

	Financing Medical Care	Looking After the Aged	Unemployment Problems	Adequate Housing
Individual & family	54%	42%	30%	33%
Local government	7	8	22	29
State government	11	19	26	17
National government	22	26	12	14
Private groups	4	2	3	—

SOURCE: Sidney Verba and Norman H. Nie, *Participation in America* (New York: Harper & Row, 1972), pp. 372-73. The actual question was: There is much talk about whose reponsibility it is to solve problems (like medical care, the aged, unemployment, housing). Which group should have the main responsibility for solving that problem— the individual and family, the local government, the national government, or the privately organized groups? (NORC, 1967.)

This general pattern was repeated in a Harris poll taken in 1972. Here the most popular choice of Table 4, individual and family solutions, was not given as an alternative, but the same pattern was evident. When asked which group should have the main responsibility for solving a particular problem, the national government was chosen as the most preferred means by a majority only in the obvious areas of foreign policy and the high cost of living (inflation). National government won a plurality for "improving the quality of life," but the support here represented only one third of the sample. In the more specific policy areas of help for the elderly, drugs, health, pollution, crime, and sanitation, state-local and private alternatives were far more popular.

Conclusion

Simply put, the answer you get depends upon the way the question is asked. The form of the question used by professional opinion analysts can greatly affect opinion description. It comes as no great surprise, then, to see that poll data can show that the welfare state has the support of an overwhelming majority, or of only a quarter of the population.

Most of the published research appears to support the view that a majority of Americans have been liberal. Yet, most of those who have published it have been liberal too. And there is a sizable body of research that holds the American people have not been liberal, in the sense of supporting the welfare state, at all. Political scientists drawing upon this latter research have argued that Americans hold an older, bourgeois liberalism, and that American values actually are conservative. In fact, this represents a much more credible reading of the poll data, as we shall soon see.

Chapter 2

Why the People Are Not Liberal*

STUDIES OF public opinion regarding public policy simply have too often relied upon the most elementary form of question. That is the simple assertion, with which respondents are asked to agree or disagree. This form of questioning leads the respondent in such a way that he tends to agree with the policy means, unless the statement is clearly an affront to deeply held values. When alternatives are not presented, the respondent is inclined to treat the assertion variety of question as a kind of broad value statement rather than as a commitment to a specific policy means.

The more useful form of question for policy (to put aside the more basic question of values) poses alternatives, or provides an open-ended format, so that the individual may respond in his own terms. Open-ended questions are preferred when spontaneous *demands* for policy are to be measured. The use of alternatives is preferred when the measurement sought is one of *support* for given policy proposals.

To answer the question whether the people are liberal, one must ask whether people favor using the national government as the primary means to plan for the general welfare. A close examination of data obtained by these question forms will be undertaken here to measure both the degree to which there is spontaneous demand among

---

*Adapted from *Public Opinion in the Welfare State*, a 1981 monograph published by the ACU Education and Research Institute. The thesis presented in this article is that liberal pollsters, using the methodology described in the preceding chapter, have produced a mountain of poll data that "prove" a false conclusion: that Americans are basically liberal in political outlook.

Americans for national governmental means to solve policy problems, and the support for such intervention when advocated by others.

Absence of Demand for Federal Action

When open-ended questions have been used in American opinion polls over the years, the data show that Americans have been primarily interested in family and individual problems. Table 5 lists the concerns spontaneously mentioned in polls of this nature over a long period of time. The general pattern is clear. Few respondents mentioned political problems as personal concerns, and most of those who did were concerned with threats of war and the

Table 5
Problems Facing Individuals

	1946	1951	1955	1959	1964	1971	1976
Family standard of living, housing	83%[1]	82%	39%	23%	19%	18%	20%
Family ill health, children problems	3	5	20	37	37	31[2]	16
Ill health for self	9	NA	NA	40	25	28	26
War, problems for peace	—	NA	NA	21	29	17	8
Unemployment, inflation	2	NA	9	11	17	24[3]	34[3]
Pollution	—	NA	NA	—	—	7	—
Political instability	—	NA	NA	1	2	5	—
Crime	—	NA	NA	—	—	5	—
No problems	5	NA	13	12	10	5	—

SOURCE: AIPO releases dated 9/11/46, 7/2/55; Albert H. Cantril and Charles W. Roll, Jr., *Hopes and Fears of the American People* (New York: Universe Books, 1971), p. 19 (AIPO, 1976); *U.S. News & World Report*, January 24, 1977, p. 66.

NOTE: Totals exceed 100% since respondents were allowed to give more than one reply.
[1]27% of the responses were for food, clothing, etc., shortages associated with World War II and rationing.
[2]7% of the responses were for family drug problems.
[3]13% unemployment, 11% inflation in 1971; 13% unemployment, 21% economic instability in 1976.

desire for peace. This pattern of personal concerns being predominant, moreover, seems to hold across many cultures.

Although Americans are primarily concerned with their homes, they can be led to focus upon broader problems. When asked what they think are problems for the *country*, as shown in Table 6, they name foreign policy issues as the most important in twenty-three of the thirty-five years for which data are available. This predominant concern was also shown in a major 1964 study, which found that of twenty-three issues tested, the five with the greatest concern were related to foreign policy.

Table 6
Problems Facing Country, 1935–76

Question: What do you think is the MOST important problem facing this country today?

TOP PROBLEMS, YEAR BY YEAR

1935: Unemployment	1960: Keeping peace
1936: Unemployment	1961: Keeping peace
1937: Unemployment	1962: Keeping peace
1939: Keeping out of war	1963: Keeping peace, race relations
1943: Winning the war	1964: Race relations, Vietnam
1947: Strikes	1965: Vietnam, race relations
1948: Keeping peace, economy	1966: Vietnam, inflation
1949: Strikes, keeping out of war	1967: Vietnam, race relations, inflation
1950: Strikes, taxes	1968: Vietnam, crime, inflation
1951: Korean War	1969: Vietnam, crime
1952: Korean War, corruption, inflation	1970: Vietnam, inflation
1953: Keeping peace	1971: Inflation, Vietnam, crime, drugs
1954: Keeping peace	1972: Vietnam, inflation
1955: Keeping peace	1973: Inflation
1956: Keeping peace	1974: Inflation
1957: Segregation	1975: Inflation
1958: Unemployment, peace	1976: Inflation
1959: Keeping peace	

SOURCE: *Gallup Opinion Index* (October 1971), pp. 3–4; (May 1971), p. 15; (July 1971), p. 5; (February 1970), p. 5; (March 1969), p. 3; *Roper Report* (July 1971), p. 1; AIPO releases dated 9/19/35, 12/1/48, 10/1/49, 3/19/50, 12/15/52, 1/1/54, 11/6/57; *Gallup Opinion Index* (October 1974), p. 17.

In the 1930s, however, problems relating to the Great Depression predominated. In the 1950s, concern over labor problems equaled concern for the Korean War; whereas race relations and the Vietnam War dominated the 1960s. By the early 1970s, inflation had begun to dominate.

Yet Table 6 should not be interpreted as proving that these problems were broadly recognized as most important. It seems very difficult to get Americans to agree on what the important problems are. Typically, fewer than one third volunteer even the most-mentioned problem, and then it is *one* problem only because the polling agency has grouped a number of generally similar responses under one heading. Each year replies range over a great variety of problems. The ranking of these problems may also differ with the section of the country polled.

There is little agreement when Americans are asked which problems should be handled by the national government, as Table 7 shows. In 1968 only Vietnam was mentioned by a majority (68 percent). The next most-often-mentioned problem (19 percent) was civil disorder.

Four years earlier, in 1964, Vietnam had also been the single policy mentioned by the greatest number of individuals, but in that year it was mentioned by only 15 percent— while the second most-mentioned problem, race relations, was mentioned by 12 percent. And, as shown under the "average" column, typically much smaller percentages mention specific problems as ones to be dealt with by the national government. Indeed, a majority did not even mention any Survey Research Center (SRC) policy *area*— except for military policy during the Vietnam War's active phase—as a national government problem.

There is a similar absence of consensus for federal action over the whole period when it comes to specific solutions to problems. When asked in 1936 what legislation they would like passed, not more than 4 percent of the respondents mentioned any single type, and 54 percent did

Table 7
Problems Facing Country, 1964, 1968

Question: As you well know, the government faces many serious problems in this country and in other parts of the world. What do you personally feel are the most important problems the government in Washington should try to take care of?

Policy Area Mentioned as Government Concern (Number of Policies)	% Mentioning Policy as Governmental Concern					
	1st Probe	2d Probe	3d Probe	Total	Highest Total[1]	Average[2]
1968						
Welfare policies (18)	13%	18%	13%	37%	16%	2.1%
Market regulation policies (11)	3	3	3	8	5	.7
Crime and social policies (11)	6	15	7	27	19	2.4
Social integration policies (5)	9	11	6	25	7	5.0
Foreign military policies (11)	45	25	12	79	68	7.2
Foreign international policies (8)	3	5	6	13	7	1.6
Other policies	6	7	6	17	8	—
No problem mentioned	2	15	47	—	—	—
1964						
Welfare policies (11)	19%	17%	9%	34%	10%	3.1%
Market regulation policies (17)	10	8	5	21	5	1.2
Crime and social policies (2)	3	2	—	5	5	2.5
Social integration policies (6)	16	8	3	28	12	4.7
Foreign military policies (15)	33	18	7	41	15	2.7
Foreign international policies (9)	7	3	2	10	5	1.1
Other policies	3	2	1	4	2	—
No problem mentioned	18	42	72	—	—	—

SOURCE: Survey Research Center/Center for Political Studies (SRC) from the Inter-University Consortium for Political Research (ICPR).

[1]This column reports the highest percentage mentioning any single policy (for example, the Vietnam War as one choice under the heading foreign military policies) within each policy area.

[2]This column reports the total percentage mentioning any policy whatever.

not mention any. In 1942 no one type of legislation was demanded by more than 19 percent of the respondents, and 47 percent had no suggestions. When asked in 1948 if there were any laws they would like to see the president support, respondents gave a wide range of replies, but 66 percent did not have any demands. In 1959 no one policy was mentioned often, and 62 percent of the respondents suggested no solution. In 1967 and 1972, replies again took many forms, yet only one fourth of the population mentioned government as a means to solve their personal problems.

This thirty-year record of reluctance (when answering open-ended questions) to demand national government action has not, unfortunately, been studied in depth with a representative national sample. One national study of men just beyond high school age, however, does use a form of open question about national priorities. The young men were first asked to rate in importance the issues of nuclear war, population growth, crime and violence, pollution, race relations, and hunger and poverty. After rating these, all were asked, "Do you have any ideas as to what should be done about this problem—by government, schools, or anyone else?" Although the question specifically suggested government as one source of a solution, on no issue did a majority demand government action: 49 percent favored government action on crime, 47 percent on pollution, 27 percent on poverty, 20 percent on population growth, 10 percent on war, and 8 percent on race relations. Most did not know if anything could be done about the threat of nuclear war, but on the other questions, nongovernmental solutions were suggested. For the social-welfare areas of poverty, population control, and race relations, large majorities suggested personal voluntary solutions.

Although the spontaneous data are limited, they all tend toward a similar conclusion. There seems to be little agreement among Americans as to what national problems other than war are important, little agreement as to how they should be solved, and *even less demand for using national government as a means for solving domestic problems.*

Tax and Redistribution Policy

Any effort to determine whether Americans are liberal, in the contemporary sense of the word, must examine welfare-state issues in more detail. Implicit in the idea of the welfare state is a redistribution of resources toward those who need welfare. But this requires prior collection of wealth or income through taxation. Although taxation takes many forms in the United States, the largest single source—and the tax best known to most Americans—is the income tax. Not only does it provide a means to redistribute wealth through welfare, but progressive rates of income taxation are themselves also a means of redistribution.

The federal income tax dates from 1913. Until the advent of the welfare state it was a very restricted form of taxation, paid by only 29 percent of households as late as 1942. Throughout the 1930s, most Americans were opposed to extending the income tax to any larger proportion of the population. In 1935, 72 percent disagreed with the proposition that everyone should pay income taxes, and in 1937, 54 percent would not agree to extend the income tax to any more families. Just before Pearl Harbor a majority supported a $10 tax for all those earning over $1,000, but 79 percent would not support any more than this token tax. Indeed, a general income tax was not broadly supported until World War II. Only after the attack on Pearl Harbor did the majority support widespread income taxes. That support lasted through the war.

Since 1945, however, Americans have typically thought income taxes too high. Table 8 shows that the proportion who have said taxes are too high has ranged from a low of 43 percent (after the major tax reduction of the period) to a high of 71 percent in 1952 and another high of 69 percent in 1969. In fourteen of the eighteen years for which data are available, a majority has thought that income taxes have been too high. On a few occasions a plurality has believed that taxes were "about right" (no more than 1 percent has ever said they are too low). Even the modest 5 percent increase in the "victory tax" during World War II and the 10 percent "surcharge" in the late 1960s were opposed by a majority in each case. In the case of a crisis, though—such as World War II—a majority was willing to wait for tax reduction.

Table 8
Support for Income-Tax Rate

Question: Do you consider the amount of federal income tax which (you have) (your husband has) to pay as too high, about right or too low? (AIPO)			
	% Say Are Too High		% Say Are Too High
1946[1]	60%	1959	51%
1947	54	1961	46
1948	57	1962	48
1949	43	1963	52
1950	56	1964	55
1951	52	1966	52
1952	71	1967	58
1953	59	1969	69
1957	61	1973	65

SOURCE: Hadley Cantril, *Public Opinion, 1935–1946* (Princeton, N.J.: Princeton University Press, 1951), p. 323, no. 97; releases dated 3/29/47 and 4/8/49; and *Gallup Opinion Index* (April 1967), p. 17; (April 1969), p. 20; (March 1973), p. 7.

[1]Question wording differs slightly. For exact wording, consult the source.

Attitudes toward government spending have tended to run parallel to feelings about taxes: in general, a majority of Americans tend to believe that the government spends too much. Given a choice between tax cuts and spending hikes as a means of economic stimulus, majorities from 1937 to 1962 have consistently favored cuts. Likewise, in 1972, when asked to choose between holding down taxes and spending on the one hand and, on the other, increasing expenditures on social programs such as aid to the poor, the aged, and schools, 54 percent chose holding spending down, while 39 percent chose increasing expenditures. To be sure, some expenditures are more popular than others, and people are therefore less willing to have these reduced.

Since taxes are collected by all levels of government in the United States, the idea of local control may also influence opinion on them. In a 1967 Gallup survey, 49 percent said their state government spent tax money more wisely than the federal government, 18 percent said the federal government spent it more wisely, 17 percent said there was no difference, and 16 percent had no opinion. A 1969 survey found that 41 percent minded local taxes least, 14 percent state taxes, and 22 percent federal taxes. In 1971 the local bias was lower, but 44 percent still said local or state taxes gave the most for the money, while 39 percent said the national government gave the most. Likewise, a large majority believed that the national government should share its revenue with state and local governments.

Since welfare-state redistribution is regarded as a national undertaking, and since taxation is a necessary prerequisite for redistribution, these data suggest a weak base of support for this aspect of welfare-state policy. They do not, however, directly measure support for redistribution, and there are some data which suggest that a majority believe that wealth is not distributed equally. One study in the 1960s found that most people in Detroit thought that certain groups in the population were rewarded better than others. Another in 1941 found that almost six Americans in ten believed rich people had too much power, and one in 1967 found two thirds saying that income differences were too great.

Realization of differences in income, however, need not lead to a belief that they should be eliminated by the national government. Indeed, the widespread belief in achievement existing in the United States could even lead to the view that income inequality is just and equitable. In this regard, Table 9 shows that even during the depression, six in ten Americans did not believe that any limits should be placed on what income a person could earn. Although this support was lower during World War II, another question showed that this absence of majority support was only temporary. When asked *in the same year* about possible limits *after* the war, six in ten then said there should not be any limit on what a person should be able to earn. More recent opinion data in the table, likewise, show that in 1969 eight in ten Americans were opposed to having everyone receive the same income.

Table 9
Income Equality

Question: Do you believe that there should be a top limit of income and that anyone getting over that limit should be compelled to turn the excess back to the government as taxes? (FOR, 1939)

Should Limit 30%
Don't Know............... 9
Should Not Limit 61

Question: After the war, do you think there should be a law limiting the amount of money any individual is allowed to earn in a year? (FOR, 1942)

Should Limit 32%
Don't Know............... 8
Should Not Limit 60

Question: Do you think there should be any limit on the amount of income...that each person should be allowed to keep per year in wartime? (AIPO, 1942)

Should Limit 47%
Don't Know............... 15
Should Not Limit 38

Question: Do you think every family in this country should receive the same income, about $10,000 a year or so? (ORC, 1969)

Favor..................... 13%
Not Sure.................. 7
Oppose 80

SOURCE: Cantril, pp. 313–14, nos. 1, 3, 6; and Joe R. Feagin, "Poverty," *Psychology Today* (November 1972), p. 108. Also see Cantril, p. 314, no. 4.

It may be supposed that support for *income* inequality would not be extended to *wealth* inequality since the average citizen has income, but not much wealth. Yet there is little support for full equality of wealth. In 1937, 62 percent said that they did not believe that inheritances should be limited. In 1939, three fourths were opposed to confiscating all wealth beyond that needed to live decently; and Table 10 shows that on two occasions during the depression, pluralities were opposed to limiting the size of private fortunes. The Detroit study mentioned above found that in 1960 two thirds were opposed to dividing wealth up equally "so that people will have an equal chance to get ahead."

Table 10
Wealth Equality

Question: Do you believe the government should limit the size of private fortunes? (AIPO)		
	1936	1937[1]
Yes	41%	44%
No opinion	9	8
No	50	48

SOURCE: Cantril, p. 1040, nos. 3, 5.

[1]The 1937 question did not say that the *government* should be the one to limit the size of fortunes. Perhaps this accounts for some differences in response.

In 1939, Americans were asked whether they thought "government should or should not redistribute wealth by heavy taxes on the rich," and a majority said that the government should not engage in such redistribution. Yet Americans do seem to believe that the rich should pay somewhat more. When asked during the depression whether "the federal government should follow a policy of taking money from those who have much and giving money to those who have little," only 30 percent said yes. On the other hand, 26 percent more would say yes "if it does not go far," while 41 percent were totally opposed. In 1935 less than a majority believed that fortunes of over one million dollars should be taxed more highly than average savings.

Although Americans often believe that the rich should pay more, the redistribution range has been narrow. In 1941 a majority said that a 50 percent tax rate was too high for a person earning $50,000 a year. In 1946 a plurality said that no one should pay a tax rate of more than 50 percent, and during the 1950s majorities supported a maximum tax rate of 25 or 35 percent. In a relatively large number of polls people were asked to specify the taxes that different income classes should pay. Interestingly, the results for the nine polls on this topic taken between 1941 and 1961 have been remarkably consistent. In all of them the public has favored lower and much less steeply graduated income-tax rates. For incomes over $50,000 the favored rate was typically 20 percent in the 1940s and early 1950s and 15 percent in the mid-1950s and early 1960s. In 1961 most believed that incomes over $100,000 per year should be taxed at only a 15 percent rate. These rates are much lower than those set for higher income categories by the political system, and it would appear, therefore, that redistribution in the United States is much less popular among the general public than among elected officials.

It is difficult to avoid the conclusion that Americans do not believe in massive redistribution of income or wealth. At the most, they believe that the wealthy should pay a modestly higher rate in line with what they are thought to be able to afford.

It seems difficult to explain this result outside the context of American political culture. The classical view of democracy has been that its egalitarian principles, together with human greed and the short-run economic interests of the poor, would lead the people to demand that the wealth of the rich be redistributed. Yet in the United States, support for the values of liberty, property, and achievement seems to have outweighed support for economic equality. In addition, Americans have a strong feeling of community which transcends economic and other social cleavages, and which leads them to believe that all should be allowed to keep the economic rewards that they have been legitimately able to obtain. When, in 1969, those earning less than $4,000 per year were asked if they favored redistributing income to give everyone an equal income of $10,000, only 14 percent were in favor.

The welfare state, however, need not be defined exclusively to include massive redistribution (although it must include some). Rather, it may imply pragmatic support for specific national programs to provide welfare for the needy. To test whether the welfare state has been popular, then, it is also necessary to look at support for programs intended to alleviate specific kinds of distress.

Medical Insurance

Health care has long been a concern of the national government, especially since 1965. Indeed, by 1977 approximately forty billion federal dollars were spent on health services—most of it on medicaid (health insurance for the needy) and medicare (health insurance for those over sixty-five). Since Table 5 showed that health concerns are important to Americans, one might suspect that support for such programs would be substantial. Table 11, moreover, shows sizable support for some type of government assistance. It is difficult to evaluate whether the sharp decline in support between 1942 and 1956 reflects an actual shift in public attitudes or a change in the form of the question; since the proportion opposed increased much less dramatically, it is more likely the latter. In any event, there has been majority support over this time period for the general idea of government involvement in medical care.

Table 11

Support for Governmental Medical Care

Question: Do you agree or disagree that the government ought to help people get doctors and hospital care at low cost?[1]

	Approve	Qualified, No Opinion No Interest	Disapprove
July 1936	74%	6%	20%
June 1937	74	7	19
May 1938	78	4	18
April 1942	74	5	21
September 1956	54	20	26
September 1960	60	20	20
September 1964	50	22	28
September 1968	52	21	27

SOURCE: Schiltz, p. 128 (SRC, 1968), ICPR.

[1]Question wording is slightly altered from year to year. For exact wordings, consult the source, pp. 191–92.

The questions in Table 11 deal with general values rather than specific programs. When questions are focused on federal involvement and when cost is mentioned, the results are quite different. Table 12 shows opinion for and against federally sponsored health insurance when the question was first considered in the 1940s. As is shown, in two cases there was an absolute majority in favor of government medical care and in three cases there was not. In two of the latter cases, opinion is almost divided between favorable and unfavorable views; in one case there is a significant plurality against government medical care.

A 1945 study found that 68 percent of the population favored extending social security to cover health insurance. However, 70 percent also said they favored a purely private solution to the problem. Since both approaches obtain majority support, it is clear that opinion can be evaluated only when the approaches are specified and contrasted. Table 13 presents a comparison. During the 1940s, when the

Table 12
Support for Governmental Medical Care and Cost

	Support for Governmental Medical Care When Tax Mentioned	No Opinion	Opposition to Taxed Medical Care
July 1943[1]	44%	16%	40%
February 1944[2]	32	26	42
August 1944[3]	57	12	31
May 1945[4]	51	11	38
April 1949[5]	45	14	41

SOURCE: Schiltz, pp. 131, 192.

[1]Actual Question: Would you be willing to pay (or have your husband pay) 6 percent of your salary or wages (or income) in order to make this program possible? (AIPO)

[2]Would you approve or disapprove of such a plan [to increase social-security taxes and have the federal government use the money for a medical and hospital insurance program]? (ORC)

[3]If this meant that 2½ percent of people's paychecks would be taken out instead of the present 1 percent, would you think this a good idea or a bad idea? (NORC)

[4]Would you favor increasing the present [social-security] tax rates to include payment of benefits for sickness, disability, doctor, and hospital bills? (AIPO)

[5]Do you think the U.S. Congress should or should not pass the government's compulsory health insurance program which would require wage (salary) deduction from all employed persons to provide medical and hospital care for them and their problems? (AIPO)

issue arose during the Roosevelt and Truman administrations, there was a clear plurality opposed to the government alternative and in favor of the private. Unfortunately, when the controversy arose again in the 1970s, the available question did not include a cost aspect, but used an interest filter that excluded part of the sample from giving an opinion, and used a complex scale technique that is difficult to evaluate in descriptive analysis. As Table 13 shows, the number in favor of national health insurance remained at the same level, but the number opposed dropped. When this question was asked in 1972, a plurality favored national health insurance—but the difference could arise from survey error.

Even this breakdown of opinion on governmental

Table 13

Governmental vs. Private Medical Insurance

	Percent for National Health Insurance and Taxation	No Opinion	Percent for Private Insurance Plan
February 1944	37%	20%	43%
July 1945	39	15	46
March 1949	33	20	47
November 1972[1]	37	31	32

SOURCE: Schiltz, p. 131 for 1944–49; SRC from ICPR for 1972.

NOTE: Question wording is slightly altered from year to year. For exact wording, consult the source, pp. 193–94.

[1]No cost criterion was used in this question. An interest filter and a semantic differential scale were also used.

medical care is overly simplified. When asked in 1946 whether they would rather have the government, private insurance companies, or the medical profession handle health insurance, 35 percent chose the government solution and 52 percent chose private solutions (31 percent insurance company, and 21 percent medical profession solutions). In 1967, when asked which group should be the main one to finance medical care, 58 percent said private groups, 18 percent said state-local governments, and 22 percent said the federal government. In 1972, 22 percent chose national health insurance, 40 percent chose government payment only for the needy, and 30 percent chose the present system.

In the 1940s, in response to an open-ended question, only about one third of the population spontaneously demanded government solutions to health-care problems (Table 14). Of those wishing government solutions, as many wanted it done by local as by the federal government. In all studies allowing for detailed responses, therefore, private and local plans and those providing assistance only for the needy have received much more support than pure national health alternatives. Even when only private and national government alternatives are contrasted, private alternatives received plurality support in the 1940s and there was no majority demand or support for a policy of national health insurance as late as 1972 (Tables 7, 13, and 14).

Table 14

Opinion on Solutions to Medical Care Problems

Question: What do you think should be done, if anything, so that people can get medical care when they need it?

NORC 1944		AIPO[1] 1946	
Nothing	10%	Nothing	9%
Government (federal, state or local)	26	Government (social security)	11
		Other national government	5
'Private medicine	42	Other government	17
Private insurance	6	Private medicine	26
Private charity	3	Private charity	2
Misc. private	5	Misc.	12
Undecided	8	No opinion, don't know	18

SOURCE: Cantril, pp. 441–42, nos. 31, 43.

NOTE: Question wording differs slightly for 1946. For precise wording, consult the source.

The question of medical care was also raised in the 1960s in the more restrictive form of care for the aged. As in Table 11, the general idea was popular; six in ten supported the general idea of health care for the aged under social security. On the other hand, when asked whether they supported an American Medical Association plan to give governmental assistance only to those aged who could not afford private insurance, 56 percent likewise supported that option. Asked to compare governmental medical care for the aged with private plans, a plurality preferred the government solution (Table 15). Yet, there is *no majority* demand or even majority support for national old-age health insurance—as there is none for universal national health insurance—during the period of the present study.

Table 15
Support for Governmental Medical Care for the Aged

	Support for Aged Medical Care Under Social Security (Tax Mentioned)	No Opinion	Support for Private Plan
March 1962	55%	11%	34%
May 1962	48	11	41
July 1962	44	16	40
February 1965	46	18	36

SOURCE: Schiltz, p. 140.

NOTE: Question wording differs slightly over time. However, each offers a choice between voluntary health insurance and social-security-taxed governmental insurance. For exact wording, consult the source, pp. 194-95.

Public Welfare

There is substantial support for aiding those who are in need. In 1965, for example, 84 percent of Americans said they felt badly that people in the United States go hungry, while two thirds said they worry that people abroad do not have enough to eat. Large majorities sympathized with those who lived in slums, and felt sorry for the way the Negro has been treated. Table 16 also shows that between seven and eight in ten Americans have consistently supported government assistance to those who have no means of making a living.

This support for altruistic values, however, must be placed in context: when costs are mentioned, support normally decreases. Thus, when subjects are asked whether they would support government welfare to the needy even if it meant higher taxes, the size of the majority in favor declines. Support for welfare declines much more drastically if people suspect that those to be aided are not really needy. When asked in 1938 whether they would pay more taxes to increase benefits to those on *relief* (rather than those in need), 87 percent said they would not. Likewise, although a

Table 16
Welfare Altruism

Question: Do you think the government should provide for all people who have no means of obtaining a living? (FOR)	
	% Support
March 1939[1]	74%
December 1939	67
September 1946	79
September 1948	80

SOURCE: Schiltz, p. 111.

[1]Question wording was slightly changed. Consult source for exact wording.

majority supported aid to veterans in general, a majority did not support an increase in taxes to pay more benefits. Support for unemployment insurance in general is not translated into support for higher taxes to give an increase in benefits. Table 17 presents data over three and a half decades on public perceptions of expenditures for welfare. For most of this period the public split widely over whether expenditures should be increased, decreased, or kept the same.

A poll in 1965 found that 43 percent viewed welfare in favorable terms, 45 percent had mixed feelings, 6 percent had no opinion, and 6 percent said the programs should be done away with. This ambivalence seems to result from the context within which people evaluate welfare. Table 18 shows that over a period of three decades a large majority has held that at least some of those on welfare cheat. In the 1965 study, 7 percent thought most recipients were dishonest, 61 percent thought some were, 17 percent thought very few were, and 3 percent thought none were. In 1969, 84 percent agreed that there were too many people receiving welfare.

Americans also tend to view welfare as a threat to the achievement value, large majorities believing that welfare and relief make people lazy, and that poverty is not wholly the result of circumstances beyond one's control, but is at

Table 17
Support for Costs of Public Welfare

| | % Saying Government Should | | | |
	Increase Expenditures for Welfare	Keep Expenditures the Same for Welfare	Decrease Expenditures for Welfare	No Opinion
October 1935	9%	31%	60%	—
April 1937	11	39	44	6%
November 1937	24	27	49	—
January 1939	24	29	39	8
January 1939	17	39	38	6
January 1940	20	24	44	12
February 1940	27	39	6	28
February 1940	23	38	9	30
January 1943	24	29	39	8
October 1961	35	33	19	13
November 1961	27	35	23	15
November 1964	18	32	20	30
June 1972	30	41	24	5

SOURCE: Schiltz, p. 152; William Watts and Lloyd A. Free, *State of the Nation* (New York: Universe Books, 1973), p. 296.

NOTE: Question wording differs greatly over the time period. For exact wording, consult the source, pp. 195–97. Two polls were omitted due to question-wording problems noted in the source and possible response-set difficulties.

Table 18
Welfare Cheating

| | % Who Say That Some on Welfare | | |
	Cheat	No Opinion	Not Cheat
August 1937	55%	30%	15%
April 1939	69	17	14
November 1964	67	12	21
August 1965	83	10	7
Spring 1969	84	5	11

SOURCE: Schiltz, p. 156; Feagin, p. 107, no. 1.

NOTE: Question wording differs significantly, ranging from believing that many (some) could find jobs if they tried to whether some are dishonest being on relief. Consult the source for the exact wording.

least partially caused by personal lack of effort. Table 19 shows that in 1964 only 29 percent (and this figure decreased 10 percent over the next three years) thought poverty was environmentally caused and nearly two thirds thought it was at least in part individually caused. In 1967 four in ten thought it was most often caused by individual failings. The table also shows that most Americans believe that some people simply are not able to rise above poverty. But for those who can, in 1964, 85 percent said that individual initiative could end poverty better than could governmental welfare programs.

Table 19

Poverty

Question: In your opinion which is more often to blame if a person is poor? (AIPO)			
	Circumstances Beyond Control	Lack of Effort	Both	No Opinion
March 1964	29%	33%	32%	66%
December 1965	29	40	28	3
June 1967	19	42	36	3

Question: Do you think poverty will ever be done away with? (AIPO)		
	Yes	No Opinion	No
August 1937	13%	4%	83%
March 1964	9	8	83
June 1967	7	4	89
March 1969	10	10	80

SOURCE: *Gallup Opinion Index* (July 1967), pp. 16-17; Joe R. Feagin, "American Attitudes Toward Poverty and Anti-Poverty Programs" (unpublished ms., 1969), p. 57.

The most important aspect of welfare opinion, however, is that Americans have made a distinction between the needy and those receiving welfare. Whereas they are favorable to the former, they disapprove of the latter. They believe that many people are on relief because they have not tried hard enough to get a job, that many cheat to stay on relief, and that individual effort could get most people off relief.

Large majorities accordingly want to make the welfare requirements stricter to force the undeserving off welfare. In 1965, for example, 69 percent wanted to make the unemployment benefit laws stricter. Table 20 shows that large majorities have believed that those on welfare who are able must work if they are to continue receiving benefits. Large majorities have favored guaranteed-work proposals (although not if taxes are increased significantly) but not the more liberal alternative of guaranteed income. Finally, most have opposed welfare plans that continue to pay benefits to unwed mothers who continue having children, and most have supported strict residency requirements to qualify for welfare aid.

Table 20
Work Requirements on Welfare

Question: All men on relief who are physically able to work must take any job offered which pays the going wage. Would you favor or oppose this plan for this area? (AIPO)

	Favor	No Opinion	Oppose
August 1961	84%	6%	10%
January 1965	84	5	11

Question: If men on relief, who are physically able to work, cannot find jobs, then they must work for the city on streets, parks, and the like. Would you favor or oppose this plan for this area? (AIPO)

	Favor	No Opinion	Oppose
August 1961	85%	6%	9%
January 1965	82	6	12

SOURCE: AIPO release dated 8/12/61; *Gallup Opinion Index* (June 1965), p. 20.

Support for welfare must also be put in the context of other cultural values. Private welfare is strongly supported, one poll showing that 69 percent of Americans have contributed to a charity and 59 percent say they would work on a local committee to solve welfare problems. Unfortunately, questions contrasting private and public welfare are not available. All available data indicate that mention of the local community makes respondents more favorable to welfare. As noted above, only about four in ten Americans seem to have favorable feelings about welfare, but a question in 1964 emphasizing *local* welfare found that 86 percent supported welfare at this level. Table 21 lists four questions posed over a twenty-five-year period which directly contrasted federal with state-local welfare, each of which found state-local alternatives better supported.

Table 21
Local Government and Welfare

	AIPO[1] 1936	FOR[2] 1937	AIPO[3] 1939	AIPO[4] 1961
Federal	45%	35%	36%	29%
State-local	55	45	64	55
Combination	—	6	—	—
None	—	3	—	—
Don't know	—	10	—	16

SOURCE: Cantril, pp. 893–96, nos. 3, 20, 35; AIPO release dated 8/11/61.

[1]Actual question: Should the responsibility of caring for all persons be returned now to the state and local governments?

[2]Actual question: Which kind of government—federal, state, or local—do you feel should take care of relief?

[3]Actual question: Do you think unemployment relief should be handled by the federal government or by state and local governments?

[4]Actual question: At present, most of the regulations dealing with persons on relief come from the state government or Washington. Would you like to have this policy continued or would you give local communities more say as to which persons should get relief and how much?

Americans, therefore, have supported the idea of aiding the needy, but have also believed that there are many things wrong with relief programs. Most Americans have supported strict means to deal with welfare problems, including a requirement that those who are physically able should work before receiving benefits. Importantly, most have also stated that welfare should be handled by local rather than by national government.

Are Americans Liberal Supporters of the Welfare State?

A detailed look at data collected over a period of many years evokes a compelling conclusion: on bellwether issues measuring support for welfare-state policies, Americans simply cannot be described as liberals.

Little support can be found among Americans for the general idea of redistributing wealth. Indeed, it appears that if the people were directly to set income-tax rates, there would be lower rates on the rich, and thus even less redistribution than the system now has. The surveys reviewed here, however, did show some support (although not spontaneous demand) for several mildly redistributive policies.

A plurality, but not a majority, has supported medical care for the aged. Opinion has been divided over national health insurance. In neither case has a majority demanded any particular means and, in fact, a plurality spontaneously mentioned private solutions to medical care problems (Table 14). A majority seems to have opposed the relief policy of the period, preferring work-oriented local alternatives.

Majority support for welfare-state policy can be demonstrated only by using assertion-type questions such as those in Tables 11 and 16. Yet because these questions omit any mention of costs or alternatives, they seem to measure not so much commitment to specific means as support for broad values. Thus, support for medical care in Table 11 and welfare in Table 16 simply seems to measure respondents' support for the value of altruism. To judge policy, there must be a measure of means, and the plainest way to make it clear that they must be evaluated is to show alternative ways to achieve the goals. When this occurs, the majority support disappears in division over different means to implement these values.

Even the more complex questions do not pose exhaustive alternatives, and different ones could change the present interpretation. The ones presented, though, do seem to be genuine alternatives, and it is doubtful that the major conclusion—that a majority of Americans have not demanded welfare-state means or policies—would be changed by other choices. At a minimum, the data derived from open-ended or question-posing alternatives should be considered more seriously than they have in the past by those who have evaluated this problem. This has not been done, even though one of the evaluators had himself previously noted that open-ended and alternative-posing forms were superior means of measuring true opinion. When questions posing alternatives have been evaluated, moreover, the implications have not been drawn. For example, one analyst stressed how large the *minority* was which supported a welfare-state policy in one case, and speculated that respondents must have been tricked for them not to have supported the welfare-state alternative in another.

It is significant that welfare concerns per se tended not to be mentioned as most important for most years during which data are available (Table 6). More important, Table 7 shows that no more than 37 percent of the people spontaneously demanded that welfare problems be handled by means of the national government. Moreover, of the alternative means of dealing with welfare problems—national government, state-local government, and private—the national alternative is the least popular. It seems nothing short of ridiculous to conclude, as did one liberal pollster, that Americans support the welfare state because most people agree that "the government should make sure that 'the poor are taken care of and that no one goes hungry.'" For political liberalism is a commitment not only to provide welfare, but also to use the means of the national government to do so.

American opinion, however, has not rallied around the national welfare-state solution. As a major study of welfare opinions in the United States has noted, the people strongly believe that they must respond to those who think they are in need, but they disagree over *how* the need should be alleviated. Certainly, there is no majority support for using the national government to redistribute income, or to assume control of major welfare programs. Indeed, state-local and private solutions seem more supported.

Chapter 3

Why the People Are Conservative*

THE AMERICAN people are conservative because a large majority support a consistent set of long-held values derived from the philosophy of John Locke and the American founders. And having investigated the public opinion poll data of the last three decades, we can only conclude that Americans still support that traditional, liberal culture. That is, the people are still conserving a liberal—in the classical sense of minimal involvement by the national government in individual lives—culture. The people are liberal in this sense, but conservative in that more fundamental and politically relevant sense.

The people identify strongly with the nation and their fellow citizens; and they are emotionally committed to common symbols of them. That is, they are patriotic. The people also give strong support to the means of their political institutions: they support their pluralist democratic regime, its three branches (especially the legislative), federalism, and decentralized political parties. Finally, they support the bourgeois values of the home, liberty, political equality, property, achievement, belief in God, religion, and altruism.

In this book, three decades of data have been reviewed. Many individual survey questions have been investigated, using language directly from the *Second Treatise* and *The*

* Adapted from my book, *The Political Culture of the United States* (Little, Brown, 1972). The poll questions focusing on current public policy issues presented in the previous chapter show that the American people reject statist solutions to economic and social problems, and prefer local government or private solutions. This chapter makes clear that they also exhibit a strong faith in traditional Western values, a hallmark of political conservatism.

Federalist Papers to provide the specific research hypotheses to be tested. In every case the attitudes of Americans seemed to fulfill the expectations of the hypothesis.

The question naturally arises whether support for the values of the tradition has changed over time. Unfortunately, it is difficult to test the hypothesis by era with the limited data available. If the questions used in this chapter were asked in the same form at set time intervals, I believe the data would show some variation in support for individual values of the tradition between eras, together with consensus support for each value and a generally stable support for all of the values considered together as a political culture.

Table 22 presents a very rough attempt to summarize support for the major values of the liberal tradition for which there are data over time. Although the summary is only approximate, and the absolute levels shown should not be taken as precise, it is probably an acceptable model of reality. The data suggest that support for the values vary but that an average of three fourths of the people support the values over time. Six of ten support each value in every era.

Support for political values does appear, then, to be consensual. But what is the nature of this support? How widespread must support be?

For the major values, 307 tests have been performed to find the extent to which Lockean values were supported by thirty-seven major social groups. Only 3.5 percent of these tests did not show majority support for the tradition values. The data may also be viewed chronologically. If the values are divided into four time groups—1940–48, 1958, 1960, 1967–68—group support does not differ significantly for the four periods. That is, there does not seem to be any trend over time, at least with these indicators, in support for the tradition.

Thirty-seven major social groups were identified. Only five groups (14 percent of the groups) showed support that fell below a majority for even one measure of the tradition.

Table 22
American Support for Traditional Values

Value	Mean Support for Values				
	1935-45	1946-55	1956-70	1971-76	1982[4]
1. National unity	—	94%	88%	87%	80%
2. Community trust	66%	66	77	67[1]	—
3. National anthem symbol	65	—	—	—	—
4. Popular rule and elections	—	86	79	91[1]	—
5. Legislative predominance	71	62	78	80	53
6. Federalism	65	—	65	72	—
7. Decentralized parties	62	69	73	56	—
8. The home	68	—	—	80	89
9. Liberty	72	72	68	81[2]	72
10. Political equality	98	—	85	—	—
11. Property	60	66	66	66[2]	69
12. Achievement	74	—	86	73[1]	84
13. Belief in God	96	95	98	94[3]	95
14. Religion	70	72	73	71[1]	71
15. Altruism	—	—	73	58[2]	—
Mean support for political culture by era	74%	76%	78%	75%	77%

SOURCE: Donald J. Devine, *The Political Culture of the United States* (Boston: Little, Brown, 1972), pp. 92, 99. For 1971-76: *Current Opinion* (May 1974), p. 50.

[1]Survey Research Center/Center for Political Studies (SRC), 1972 *Election Study* from Inter-University Consortium for Political Research (ICPR): *Gallup Opinion Index* (December 1973), p. 12; *Confidence and Concern: Citizens View American Government* (Washington, D.C.: Senate Subcommittee on Intergovernmental Relations, 1973), p. 66; *Gallup Opinion Index* (February 1975), p. 15; Institute of Life Insurance Poll in *Current Opinion* (June 1974), p. 64.

[2]Harris poll in *Current Opinion* (October 1973), p. 102.

[3]AIPO (Gallup) poll in *Current Opinion* (August 1976), p. 85.

[4]1982 data from Center for Applied Research in the Apostolate: questions 163, 274, 348, 349, 135, 246.

Apoliticals constituted the only group that did not support the political culture. This is not a surprising finding. In the political specialization of labor the apoliticals have removed themselves from the political system. This 5 percent of the population has become irrelevant in regard to policy. It is not a meaningful exception to the general finding that American tradition is supported by all relevant potential cleavages. This observation of weak support by those unrelated to politics also helps explain a pattern of support among other groups. Not only do Republicans, Democrats, and Independents support more highly than apoliticals, but attentives support more than nonattentives; upper and middle classes support more than the lower; the highly educated support more than the less; the middle-aged support more than either the young or the old; and whites support more than blacks. The groups more specialized toward politics are more supportive of the political culture. Again, this pattern does not mean that the less politically oriented groups do not support the tradition. Every group (except the apoliticals) supports the liberal tradition as the political culture of the United States.

In sum, whether one considers political, economic, ecological, or other societal groupings, there is a wide consensus across American society. Of course, not every conceivable group in the American system positively supports the tradition. Some smaller groups are probably ambivalent and accept the regime only by sufferance. The data do suggest additivity of these dimensions. For example, 90 percent of all American system members support popular control, while 68 percent of the low education group (zero to seven years of schooling) support the value and 60 percent of the apoliticals do. The group that is both less educated and apolitical, however, shows support of only 44 percent.

Other groups undoubtedly actually reject the regime and its value system. For example, 76 percent of college students who call themselves revolutionaries reject traditional American values. Very likely other small groups do too. In considering groups smaller than the general potential social cleavages, however, one is no longer dealing with mass support. Politically relevant groups composing less than 1 percent of the population should be considered as low-level elites. Actually, support by political elites may be more important for regime maintenance than mass support.

At the mass level, for both the masses and their major social groupings, the liberal tradition is supported as a consensual political culture. Although one could never, in some absolute sense, demonstrate the existence of the liberal tradition as the political culture of the United States, I will argue that the widespread agreement on political values reported above and the depth of support shown here represent a reasonable empirical demonstration of support for our institutions. The Lockean tradition may be used as an empirical description of the political culture of the United States. In that sense, Americans are conservative. They have conserved that value system for two centuries, in spite of massive political change over that period of time.

Part II

The Politics

Chapter 4

A Four-Year Strategy for Conservative Victory*

ALTHOUGH THE presidential election was closer than some had earlier expected, it is clear that the 1976 election was a disaster for the Republican party. In the House, the Republicans were reduced to essentially the number they had after the 1964 election. There were fewer only in the depression years of 1932 to 1936.

For state-level elections, the Senate is somewhat more congenial for Republicans, although even here the strength is below average. This glimmer of hope is narrowed when one considers that 75 percent of the nation's governors are Democratic and, as impossible as it sounds, even more states have their legislatures controlled by the Democrats. And, of course, the Republicans lost the presidency.

More important, the decline seems to be of a long-term nature. Republican representation in the House, accordingly, has been on the wane since the early 1950s. In addition, those from the population at large who consider themselves Republican have fallen from 40 percent in 1940 to 30 percent in 1960 to roughly 20 percent in 1976.

*Reprinted from *Human Events,* November 20, 1976. Although, as we have seen, the people are conservative, the Republican party repeatedly failed to emphasize conservative values and issues in seeking public support. Following Ronald Reagan's defeat in the battle for the 1976 GOP nomination, conservative leaders vowed not to allow "pragmatic" middle-of-the-roaders to delay the necessary reform of American politics by losing another election in 1980. I composed this working paper, laying out a strategy for nominating a movement conservative candidate, shortly after the 1976 presidential election. The paper was presented at a meeting organized by the American Conservative Union. At the time, one group of conservatives was demanding the creation of a new third party. I argued that conservatives should stay in the Republican Party and elect Ronald Reagan chairman.

Moreover, the decline has been most severe among the young, so the future hardly offers encouragement.

The pattern now is set so deeply that even traditional Republican strongholds show decreasing party registration. In such areas as Nassau and Suffolk counties in New York more Democrats than Republicans have registered in the past year, while of the forty-two counties where Republicans have dominated registration in the past in Pennsylvania, recent registration has favored the Democrats in thirty-three. Likewise, in the former Republican stronghold of Polk County (Des Moines), Iowa, registration has been running four-to-one Democratic over the past year.

The usual conclusion drawn from these data is that the Republican party is dead. Yet, one should be careful to go that far since both the Democratic and Republican parties have been declared moribund many times; and, as Mark Twain said about himself, the reports of death have been greatly exaggerated.

American parties have been considered prematurely dead so many times because prognosticators always underestimate the resilience of both parties in an always adapting two-party system. In such a system, and especially for the big prize of the presidency, there is an ebb and flow of failure and then success as the candidates of each party are able to exploit the mistakes made by the other party.

It is likewise unappreciated that candidates have great effect upon party images so that past unpopularity can be adjusted in the reflection of a new personality and new issues which provide the possibility for a revitalization of the previously defeated party.

It is in this context that the current position of the Republican party must be evaluated if one is to have a rounded picture. Thus, while it is true Gallup polls show that only 20 percent of the people believe Republicans can solve political problems better than can Democrats, this was also so in 1962, 1968, and 1971, following which Republicans won two presidential elections. Again, while Republicans were down to 144 seats in the House in 1974–76, they were down to about that many in 1936 and won eighty seats back in the next election. And the same rebound occurred after 1958 when twenty seats were won in 1960 and after 1964 when almost fifty seats were recaptured in 1966.

To balance this, though, one must note that the long-term trend has been on the ebb and that the present low level of congressional representation has existed now for two successive elections. Conditions do change and it is certainly possible the Republican party is in a permanent decline.

The alternative to the Republican party, of course, is a new conservative party. Yet, this alternative has costs which make its viability questionable. Ballot qualifications and electoral laws differ in each state to such a degree that great time, expense, personnel, and expertise must be spent in mastering and complying with them. About all the rules have in common is that they make it difficult for new parties.

Only two states allow third parties to add their votes to those of another party, so that the party may begin by endorsing some of a major party's candidates. This is an important limit to the ability of third parties to grow slowly in strength over time. Without this legal option being available in New York, its Conservative party could not have reached its present position of political power. Not only do state laws work against new parties but the recent national campaign "reforms" do likewise, especially in the critical problem of financing. So a new party starts with all the rules of the game biased against it and in a less favorable financial situation.

A new party, then, must convince an already skeptical citizenry to identify with and then support the new party. But it will find itself trapped by the historic circularity that the new party cannot show the people it is any better than the two major parties (which do make appealing *promises*) unless it obtains power but that it cannot obtain power until it proves itself.

The same reluctance to back a new party may be said to exist among party volunteers, technicians, and present party and public officials, except that they will have even deeper-seated social and psychological investments in the present party structure. Consequently, few voters, workers, or leaders will switch and the new party will have to be built with new voters. This will guarantee that real change will take a generation at the least.

Moreover, several "conservative" parties already exist and these must be coopted or replaced by a new coalition if the new party is to succeed. The cooption alternative was already attempted by the Viguerie-Rusher-Phillips group at the American Independent party convention in 1976. It was such a failure that Viguerie himself admitted "any effort to organize a new majority party has been seriously set back." But the real problem with this strategy of reconciling Republicans and many of the various third-party adherents was pinpointed by one of his associates who remarked that "we're conservative, but these people are something else."

The most systematic attempt to build the new coalition has been made by *National Review*'s William Rusher and in an even more detailed way by Prof. Thomas Ireland of the University of Missouri. Ireland's formulation is to build the new party with a 10 percent economic conservative base added to a 25 percent Wallace-social conservative, a 10 percent ethnic conservative and a 10 percent functional conservative vote. However, all of these figures seem very wrong.

In the first place, it is not clear what a "functional" conservative is, since it was defined as anti-governmental bureaucracy, anti-taxes, Friedmanite, libertarian and non-religious. But the first three categories seem overlapping if not synonymous with economic conservatism and the strength of the non-Republicans in the fourth can be judged by the small size of the Libertarian party vote in 1976. And it is doubtful that the last group represents much of a conservative constituency.

According to the most reliable poll data, about 10 percent of the population is nonreligious to the extent that they do not pray at least once a week so this may constitute the whole group. But half of this group actually voted for McGovern—the highest percentage of any group to vote for McGovern except for Negroes and Jews. In addition, many who voted for Nixon were favorable to government having more power and, thus, presumably should not be counted with the other groups.

"Ethnic conservatives" were also not clearly distinguished from economic and social conservatives as many of the groups named supported Wallace or Goldwater. Indeed, the groups mentioned only total to 12 percent of the population: Italians 4 percent, Polish 2 percent, French and Gallic 2 percent, East European 1 percent and Eastern Orthodox 3 percent. Again, not all of these are by any means conservatives as large proportions in all of these groups except Eastern Orthodox voted for McGovern.

The social conservative group is likewise overestimated as a Gallup poll was used which showed that at his high point in the 1968 election, Wallace was supported by 21 percent of the electorate. Yet not only is the maximum Wallace strength used, but it is "rounded" to 25 percent rather than to 20 percent. And, finally, the economic conservatives are under-estimated.

Thus, it is said that the economic conservative strength is related to the Goldwater vote less the "die-hard" regular Republican vote and the former is arbitrarily set at 10 percent. Yet a Gallup poll of July 1, 1964 (before the Republican nomination) showed that Goldwater had the support of 18 percent of the electorate. That is, economic conservatives are underestimated by one-half, using Ireland's criterion.

Even more troubling to the traditional ("economic") conservative is what the new party would stand for. With Rusher, the program appears rather traditional, although major principles are conceded. With Ireland it is less clear but he is pragmatic enough to say that the new party should not take a position on abortion, for example, because of his fear that it would lose a percent or two for the new party coalition. In light of this, one must ask whether the new party would be even as principled in its program as the Republicans in their platforms of 1964, 1968, and 1976.

To the extent that the major proponent of a new party—author Kevin Phillips—does offer a program, however, it is even more disturbing.

Phillips says that conservatives must give up their antiquated ideas of economic freedom to attract the "majority" middle who desire government redistribution to themselves rather than to the poor. Thus, he believes that the New Deal was the ideal coalition because it redistributed from the top to the middle and that policy only went astray when "liberals" began redistributing from the middle to the poor. The new party, consequently, should support middle-class welfare, control of the economy, subsidies to business when this gives security to the new majority, and regulation of the liberals' power in the media.

Phillips even says the constitutional principle of separation of powers is "outmoded." That is, traditional conservatives are asked to give up what they have defined as conservatism in the past in order to achieve power for the new "conservative" party. Certainly, this is too high a price for most conservatives.

Contrast this pragmatism or rightwing populism with the present structure of the Republican party. The Republican party not only has ballot qualification, a firm financial base and a favorable legal status in all fifty states as well as an in-place mechanism with tens of millions of supporters and millions of workers, but it also is relatively conservative in the traditional sense of the term.

Importantly, study after study has shown that national conservatives represent a large majority of Republican activists, contributors, convention delegates, national committeemen and committeewomen, and voters. Not all are true philosophical conservatives, but between economic conservatives (18 percent of the 1964 vote), more pragmatic regular-Republican conservatives (12 percent of the vote), and social conservatives who are willing to go along on economic policy in return for social policy programs economic conservatives already support (9 percent of the 1964 vote), conservatives represent the overwhelming majority of the Republican voters. Even if one looks at the atypical 1972 election, conservatives represented two thirds of the Nixon vote.

Effective power in the Republican party, however, is better looked at within the party organization. Here the strength has been at least two-to-one conservative. Thus, in the 1972 convention battle between moderate-liberals and conservatives over apportionment, the conservatives received two thirds of the vote both in the Rules Committees and on the floor.

Likewise, in the National Committee debate over "positive action" quota-type rules, conservatives succeeded in turning a mandatory plan into a voluntary one. This took place even though the liberals had previously stacked the preliminary ("Rule 29") committee which submitted the draft plan upon which the vote was taken. In 1976, conservatives were so strong at the convention that the conservative positions on Rules and Platform were hardly challenged.

It is true that even with this strength in the party, conservatives still tend to lose when it comes to making policy—as the Nixon and Ford presidencies make clear. The reason for this, however, is simple. Conservatives do not organize their strength and they let the one-third minority control the agenda of what shall be discussed.

But if conservatives cannot control the agenda of a party where they represent two thirds of the total, how can they expect to do so in a new party where, by the Ireland estimate, they would not even constitute a majority?

It comes as a surprise to learn from various studies that what has attracted voters and activists most to the Republican party over these years has been its general philosophy of government and its foreign policies. This was true even in its worst election year, 1964—and this is attested to by studies done by moderate-liberal Republicans as well as by the present research—although the influence of principles was somewhat mitigated in 1976 by Ford's inability to communicate the platform's domestic philosophy and because of Kissinger's nontraditional foreign policy.

But if the principles expressed in its platforms were the most attractive aspect of the Republican party, it is clear that the party has not exploited them. The reason for this seems to be that the party has been dominated by elected public officials rather than by party leaders.

Public officials have two great incentives not to emphasize philosophy: (1) they are elected to represent all of the people, not just their party; and (2) they, of necessity, have to be involved in compromise if they are to be effective in the political process. Yet, as they become more enmeshed in the day-to-day, pragmatic bargaining process, they come to think of philosophy as too idealistic, as unrealistic, and they often become too willing to trade some of it for short-term advantage.

This situation cannot be eliminated completely by electing better public officials because it is in the nature of their positions to compromise. In fact, society needs some of this. But society also needs some institution to uphold principles and in democracies this is supposed to be the political party.

The leaders of the Republican party for the period of its decline since 1932, however, have not performed this function. With very few exceptions, party chairmen have been either public officials, or technicians who have followed the lead of public officials and especially of the president or minority leaders of the House and Senate.

Although this practice has existed over the whole period, it is most critical to remember how and under whose leadership this practice was institutionalized.

Following the 1964 election, a group of younger Republican members of the House of Representatives organized a successful coup to oust the incumbent minority leader using the poor performance in that election as justification. When the new leadership took power, the new minority leader announced that thereafter the Republicans in the House would no longer be dogmatic but would present pragmatic solutions to the problems raised by the Democrats. The program was called "Constructive Republican Alternative Policies." Its opponents referred to it by its initials.

Although the data rather clearly show that the Republican philosophy was one of the few positive aspects of the preceding campaign, and that the after-effects of the Kennedy assassination and Goldwater's poor performance as candidate were the major reasons for the 1964 disaster, the general perception was otherwise.

So when the normal cyclical balance returned to some degree in 1966 with a Republican gain of forty-seven seats in the House, the new leadership claimed the success was a result of its new strategy of pragmatism. The strategy then became the program for the entire party. As a result, the pragmatic leaders prospered, many to become senators and cabinet officials. One even became president.

The 1976 election defeat of President Ford, however, is a direct result of the failure of the 1965 program of former Minority Leader Ford. Since the 1966 election (which must be viewed as an equilibrium-reestablishing one), this program has been so successful that it has cost forty seats in the House and equivalent losses at every level of electoral activity. It, additionally, has led the Republican party to the point where its strongest asset, its philosophy, has been repudiated by its own leadership.

At a time when the American people have become increasingly conscious of their conservatism, the Republican party is in decline. It is argued here that this is because through word and deed the party has turned its back on its principles. In a word, although its platforms have presented its philosophy, the leaders resist and emphasize their pragmatism. Indeed, a Senator Muskie can ask a conservative Republican chairman of the Council of Economic Advisers to "explain why we need a $52-billion deficit" because he wants "to have that answer in the record for this conservative administration."

Not surprisingly, the people do not believe the Republicans uphold their philosophy any more. Thus, Harris can report, for Republicans as well as Democrats, 87 percent of Americans say that their leaders promise tax relief before elections but they do nothing about it after elected. That is, they become "pragmatic" until the next election.

This situation demands drastic reform if the people are to have a mechanism within which they can express their conservatism. If a new party is now too costly in time, money, legal disadvantages, manpower and principles (as it is), a radical change, however, can immediately be made within the Republican party.

It should begin with the name. The party should be rechristened the Conservative Republican party. A name change, though, cannot be cosmetic but must come as a result of and be perceived as a reform forced upon the party as a means to redirect the whole party machinery toward fulfillment of its principles. Perhaps a convention for this purpose should be called for 1978 so that the reform could be fought out by the entire party within the political arena for the nation to observe.

This change in direction will likewise demand the election of a new party chairman. It would be no reflection on the incumbent, who actually has been a decent chairman, but the change must start at the top. The foremost requirements of this new party leader are that he or she be capable of communicating the party philosophy and that he or she not hold elective public office. The new party rules now require that the chairman be a full-time, paid position so public officials are now automatically excluded. The requirement that the position be paid, moreover, allows the recruitment of the most able leader available.

With a new name and the new emphasis implied by this change as well as a chairman committed to these reforms and able to communicate them, the Conservative Republican party can begin to build itself toward majority status. The key to victory, really, is quite simple. To build to the 50 percent plus one majority (more or less) needed for victory, one needs to hold the 18 percent economic conservatives, the 12 percent regular (moderate-to-conservative) Republicans, and the 9 percent Wallace-type social conservatives won in 1964. To this, then, must be added the remaining 12 percent (21 percent maximum Wallace vote less 9 percent received in 1964) of social conservatives who can provide the necessary majority for victory.

To obtain this additional 12 percent, further, it is not necessary to give up traditional "economic" conservatism but merely to emphasize the social issues which this group is interested in and, when necessary, to show the group that the solutions it desires can be achieved using means compatible with traditional conservatism.

To be sure, this is not a simple task, but with intelligent

leadership which can communicate to the people, it can be done. But it can be done only if resources are concentrated where they can have effect—and for the foreseeable future this means the Republican party. Or should we say the Conservative Republican party?

Chapter 5

Preparation for the Campaign*

AN HISTORICAL opportunity is upon us. We political scientists tend to see American history divided into political eras. Indeed, we believe there have been only six of them in all of American history, the last one being the New Deal period beginning in 1932. Each of these eras has been dominated by the ideas of one party, although the other party may elect an occasional president. In this way, the Democratic New Deal has dominated American politics from 1932 to the present.

But that period is drawing to a close. At the end of each such era, the dominant party runs out of ideas. Such is the case with the Democrats today. Democratic political scientists, and even Democratic senators, are now saying that their party has run out of ideas. Today it is the conservatives who have the new ideas. The New Deal is tired and simply needs a push for it to take its place in our historical past.

Jimmy Carter only makes the change somewhat easier. Mr. Carter claims that he is a man of peace and that the conservatives want war; but the people are becoming weary of that old tune and are beginning to suspect that weakness in foreign policy leads to war, not the reverse. Mr. Carter

---

*In early 1979, conservatives from around the country gathered at the annual Conservative Political Action Conference in Washington, D.C. Their decades-long quest for a "conservative movement" conquest of the White House seemed at hand. But divisions had appeared in the ranks with attractive conservative candidates for president. In my address to the conference, I argued that our time had come, but that we had to band together. And the only way to do so was to agree upon one candidate. He should be a seasoned political veteran with a track record indicating he could win a national election, and longstanding dedication to the conservative cause. We were on the verge of a great victory—if only we could remain a united political force.

tells the people that no one can handle the impossible job of president; but the people expect that the job be done better than he has handled it. Certainly they believe that the economy can do better than a 10 percent level of inflation. The American people have just about had it with Mr. Carter's incompetence and the Democratic Congress's sorry record of performance.

So, historical conditions are set, and the dominant party has a weak incumbent. But history also teaches us that the other side must be ready. Fortunately, conservatives are ready. The organizers of this conference have prepared the way. *Human Events* provided the first, and still provides the essential communication link for movement activists. *National Review* and the other conservative journals of opinion, too, have helped us sharpen the issues. Young Americans for Freedom and the American Conservative Union have provided the political muscle. In hundreds of units around the nation, conservative activists have been busy preparing—in many cases for twenty years—for this moment.

Since the election of 1976, conservatives have focused their attention on the Republican party as their vehicle for leading the nation. The momentary flirtation with third parties has been forgotten. We have built, from the precinct to the national convention, a party that is ready for us to lead. It is still dominated by its me-too moderate faction; but the way has been prepared.

Conservative organization and the promotion of ideas have provided the means by which we have changed the popular mood. Although the American people have never really deserted their conservative political roots, their opinions have not been deeply formed and Democratic representatives of the New Deal have been able to confuse them. Conservative organizations and media have helped end that confusion. And the Carter failure now makes it manifest to all. Public opinion polls show that the term *conservative* is at an all-time high of popularity. And a review of issue after issue in opinion polls shows that the popular issues today are the conservative issues.

Very important, a conservative leader is available. Ronald Reagan has a long history of identification and involvement with the conservative movement and, indeed, with this conference. He reads *Human Events* and *National Review*, and endorses the activities of the Young Americans for Freedom and the American Conservative Union. For a decade he has been on the front line for conservative principles. He knows the issues and he knows how to communicate them.

Critically, for the first time in modern history, the beginning of a presidential campaign finds a conservative the most popular candidate for the Republican nomination. Barry Goldwater achieved this distinction, but too late: only just before the convention, when divisions within the party had become very deep. Governor Reagan today stands with about 30 percent support among Republicans, while Gerald Ford has 25 percent support. However, as the closeness of this division shows, if conservatives divide, the moderates may well win the nomination.

There are other good conservatives who could have some claim on the nomination. Yet, they have not paid their dues the way Ronald Reagan has. Ronald Reagan is the person for the time.

There seems to be some great necessity on the part of many conservatives to run after windmills, when the guns are firing on the front line. We flirted with third parties and now we are beginning to divide before the upcoming nomination. This is not the time to run away and fight another day.

The danger is internal. Not from the moderate Republicans, not from the Democrats, but from you and me. We cannot afford to divide and let the other side conquer.

We have never before been in the position we conservatives find ourselves in today. We have an excellent chance, if we unite, and if we understand what the crucial role of a political party is: rallying around the candidate with the right views who is best able to win. Cooperation, especially at critical historical moments, is essential if a movement is to achieve victory. The time is now to unite and win; to fulfill the promise of two decades of conservative activism; to set the stage for the next era in American history: the conservative era.

Chapter 6

The Nomination Struggle: Establishment vs. Grass Roots*

A CLASSIC battle between leadership and grass roots is developing in the Republican contest for president.

Republican elites in government, politics, industry, commerce, labor and the arts want John Connally for president. Howard Baker is their second choice. These are followed by Ronald Reagan, George Bush, Gerald Ford and Jim Thompson. The findings are based upon a poll (Table 23) taken by the highly respected magazine *U.S. News & World Report*.

But rank-and-file Republicans have a very different ranking of presidential candidates. In a study conducted at about the same time by the Gallup poll, Reagan was the first choice. He was followed by Ford, Connally, and Baker.

The division lines are apparent from these results. The leadership establishment prefers more moderate-to-liberal candidates like Connally, Baker, and Bush. And the grass roots prefers more conservative candidates like Reagan and Ford.

Although Connally now calls himself a conservative, and has been pictured by the media as one, his credentials are questionable at best. He was a lifetime New Dealer until he

*Reprinted with permission from *Human Events*, May 12, 1979. Divisions among conservatives were not the only obstacle facing the Reagan campaign. The same GOP "establishment" which narrowly had denied Reagan victory back in 1976 was supporting a range of candidates anxious to grab the nomination if Ronald Reagan were to falter. These establishment politicians still did not appreciate the profound transformation that had taken place in American politics since the Goldwater defeat in 1964: the stage was now set to translate the intrinsic American cultural conservatism which had been there all along into a political victory that would transform the landscape and begin a new era.

Table 23
1980 GOP Presidential Preferences

Question: Whom would you like to see nominated as the GOP candidate for president in 1980?			
	Gallup Poll of Republican Identifiers		U.S. News Poll of Republican Elites
Reagan	31%	Connally	32%
Ford	26	Baker	18
Connally	12	Reagan	11
Baker	8	Bush	11
Percy	3	Ford	8
Crane	2	Thompson	4
Thompson	2	Crane	4
Anderson	2	Anderson	3
Bush	1	Kemp	2
Others/DK	13	Others	7
	100%		100%

was picked by Richard Nixon for secretary of the Treasury. In this role as economic spokesman, he was virtually alone in advocating the very unconservative policy of wage and price controls. He also pushed for United States cooperation in an international corporative-state-type cartel to set world prices for basic commodities.

Connally does sound conservative on foreign policy. At the same time, he is advocating mandatory government service for all eighteen-year-olds. This is modeled upon the discredited Franklin Roosevelt idea of a Civilian Conservation Corps, opposed by conservatives at the time, and upon the scandal-ridden Comprehensive Employment and Training Act. The creation of a monstrous, nationwide bureaucracy for youth does not sound like a conservative program.

So the battle lines harden. Ronald Reagan clearly is a conservative. His statements and record on both foreign and domestic policy unquestionably put him in that camp. His support comes from the conservative mass base of the Republican party. John Connally obtains his support from the moderate-liberal-pragmatic wing of the party, which has its strength among the party elite in the large corporation and governmental sectors of society.

A mass-versus-elite struggle in a democracy is a dramatic one. It pits organization and electoral skills against media and boardroom and old-school-tie networks. As the election heats up, it will be interesting to see which is the stronger force in the Republican party. If the Republicans are as strong for the 1980 election as they look and if this election is as critical for the future of American politics as it now appears, this mass-elite contest will decide the direction of policy for the next generation.

Chapter 7

A Winning Strategy for Ronald Reagan*

TO: MR. WILLIAM J. CASEY and Dr. Richard P. Wirthlin.
From: Dr. Donald J. Devine.
Subject: Strategy and Targeting for November Election.

Good political strategy is like a good suit. It is measured according to the numbers, but it is tailored to the customer. So with presidential campaigns, past statistics, and presidential candidates. Likewise, neither is very useful unless shown.

This memo is, therefore, in response to your request at the Los Angeles meeting to comment upon strategy for the election. To put these in context, you should know something about me. I hold a Ph.D. in political science from Syracuse University, and have taught at the University of Maryland for thirteen years. I have written three books on American values and public opinion, and many articles on beliefs, election, and strategy. In 1976, as a director of the American Conservative Union, I wrote the in-house plan to elect Ronald Reagan in 1980. As a result of this background, I was asked by the previous campaign leadership to coordinate a long-term planning team to prepare for the fall.

Planning starts with assumptions. Unlike some of the planning discussed at our meeting, I do *not* assume: a

---

*Reprinted from *Human Events,* July 5, 1980. I had long held the view that an effective election strategy for a conservative presidential candidate would emphasize not only the traditional Republican vote, but that of the blue-collar worker who could swing traditional Democratic districts the other way. I outlined this strategy in the memo reprinted here. Surveys later showed that the coalition suggested in this strategy memo was, in fact, the one that emerged on election day.

campaign is "national," or that larger states should get a disproportionate share of resources on that criterion alone, or that Senate and House races should affect Reagan's essential strategy. Rather, I assume a presidential election must be based upon its own priority of states, whatever their size, which will contribute to 270 electoral votes; and that these states tend to fall in a regional pattern.

A presidential survey must begin with the candidate. Ronald Reagan's strategy must differ from, say, George Bush's. Reagan's strengths are: (1) he is from, known to, and understood by the West—which tends Republican in presidential elections anyway; (2) Reagan is a conservative Republican, which gives him a natural base of 20 percent of the electorate (or 40 percent of the necessary majority); (3) Reagan strikes a responsive chord in the New South, which evokes conservatism and a frontier spirit; (4) Reagan's primary victories in Democratic crossover states like Illinois and Wisconsin show he has an uncanny ability to appeal to blue-collar, ethnic, and Catholic (BCEC) voters who traditionally have voted Democratic.

Reagan Electoral Geography

The electoral-college geography which follows from these strengths rests upon four regions. The first, in basing strategy rather than in targeting, is the West. It consists of the sixteen states taken by Ford in 1976, and of 117 electoral votes. It is the essential home base which we must assume we will win, for without this premise no victory is possible. We must work these states, but it is fundamental for clear-thinking strategy to know we will win the West.

The second base is created from the solid Republican states of New Hampshire, Vermont, Indiana, Oklahoma, and Virginia. These total forty electoral votes. Again, we must know we will win these with solid state campaigns.

Third, one must add to the base the Frontier South, consisting of Texas, Mississippi, Louisiana, and Florida for sixty more electoral votes. These are more problematical, but all were lost by less than 3 percent in 1976—and both the candidate and the party are stronger now and the opposition is weaker. So, we should win these too.

These give a base vote of 217 electoral votes, leaving only fifty-three for victory. To this base must be added the target Northern Belt region where the BCEC voter lives. It represents a "belt" running from Illinois to Ohio, Pennsylvania, Maryland, and New Jersey. All of these states, too, were within 3 percent in 1976. They represent 105 electoral votes, of which we have to win only half. The belt can even be expanded to two more peripheral states, one to the west (Wisconsin, ten electoral votes) and one to the east (New York, forty-one electoral votes); but these latter are not central. Targeting the five other states is essential.

The West must be worked extremely hard at the state level. Each state must have adequate organizational budgets. California, especially, must be given strong funding. Yet, California must not set the tone for the election, certainly a problem for a largely California-based campaign. It should get disproportionate organizational funding, but not candidate time or media spending. With strong organizational efforts, the West will be won.

The strong Republican states must be handled much like the West. Adequate organizational budgets must be approved and volunteer efforts must be initiated at the state level. Here, the Republican party organizations can be utilized more because they are stronger than in many of the western states. This means fewer resources need be spent by the Reagan for President Committee (RFP). With this effort, the people will rally to their party, and we will win these states.

The Frontier South is less secure; yet it too will be won. A CBS/*New York Times* exit poll on election day 1976, using panel-test comparisons, found in a Ford vs. Carter and a Reagan vs. Carter race, Reagan would have won 4 percent more votes than Ford—enough to win all these states. Carter is weaker today, so Reagan will win bigger in 1980.

Since the presidential candidate himself should focus upon the central target, ideally, the vice presidential nominee should come from the next most vulnerable region, the South. Yet, there is no candidate who can help: both Connally and Baker do not add votes; and there is no one else. Realistically, then, there must be a very sustained national effort to recruit prominent surrogate speakers for Reagan from the South, especially Democrats from these states.

The key to changing votes here is the frontier spirit of this last-settled and most economically dynamic part of the South. This spirit is similar to the western one, so Reagan has a natural appeal. This can be aided by themes stressing productivity, lower taxes, free enterprise, etc. A nonsouthern vice president with these values could fill in with the surrogates.

Extensive organizational budgets, beyond simple electoral vote weights, and sophisticated southern and frontier spirit policies and appeals could even spill over into Tennessee (ten electoral votes) and Missouri (twelve electoral votes) as collateral—but not essential—additions to the four key states in the Frontier South region.

The battleground region for the campaign is the Northern Belt. This region must target the tone for the election, without eroding support in the other regions. Our success here will decide whether we will win. These states and their relationship with the other regions, however, present a sophisticated appeals problem, for there are three elements. There is a strongly conservative base vote of 40 percent, a moderate-Republican-Independent vote of 25 percent, and a Democratic BCEC vote of 35 percent within a majority coalition. Each item must be meshed together to win.

How Not to Win the Battleground: East to West Strategy

The 1968 Nixon campaign is an object lesson on how to try to lose an election which was won on Labor Day. The constant temptation is to win all fifty states. As a participant in strategy in 1968 (although in a relatively minor capacity), I saw this always rocking the Nixon strategy in a constant search for the moderate voter. At the end, Nixon was overscheduled into New York and Pennsylvania (which were less winnable in 1968 than in 1980) because of their large electoral votes. Michigan, Minnesota, Missouri, and Tennessee also are states which "tempt" deflection from a coherent strategy.

No state should be conceded. But neither should peripheral states distort the main strategy. The target should always be kept in sight. New York will be a very tempting target in 1980, especially with the present discontent among Jewish voters. Yet, Israel is one of the few policies Carter can influence tremendously as election day nears. With one stroke (suppose he successfully concluded a deal with King Hussein on his last visit), the entire campaign could be rocked if New York is a central component of the strategy.

The temptation is to look west to Illinois from New York. Being originally a New Yorker myself, I always keep in mind the *New Yorker*'s cover map of the United States. A very large part of the country's map is occupied by New York City (Manhattan, actually), there are a few monuments in Washington, D.C., two tall buildings in Chicago, and a movie colony in Hollywood. Otherwise, America is a deserted wasteland.

Battleground Targeting West to East

The only way to look at a Reagan targeting strategy for the Northern Belt is from Illinois to New Jersey, with New York and Wisconsin as bonuses. Indeed, we need only half of the nonbonus states' electoral vote at that. Within these five states, the hard-core *conservatives* can be consoled and even energized by basic adherence to Governor Reagan's traditional issues. The only possibility of losing this vote is a perceived "sell-out." These people will be the base of the volunteers needed for the work of the campaign. So they need continuing reassurance.

Moderate Republicans (and Democrats) cannot be assumed to vote for Ronald Reagan. John Anderson is the immediate problem, but not voting is another difficulty. Although Roper's June poll shows Carter losing 7 percent to Anderson and Reagan 6 percent, the more reliable Gallup poll shows Reagan losing 9 percent and Carter only 7 percent to Anderson. I challenge the conventional wisdom that Anderson is primarily a threat to Carter. A significant effort must be made toward these voters; if not, Pennsylvania, Maryland, Illinois, New Jersey, and probably Ohio (in that order) may be lost in November. Anderson cannot win, but he can spoil it for us among moderate Republicans. Our weakness among WASP, upper-middle-class suburban Republicans was demonstrated in the primaries in these states.

If the vice presidential candidate is not chosen from the moderate wing of the Republican party, attracting this group will be especially difficult. If George Bush is not the nominee, both he and Howard Baker should be assigned to win over these voters. They and other prominent moderates (governors, senators, etc.) must be speaking constantly to Republican gatherings aiming their appeals to this audience, without alienating the conservatives.

Unlike past campaigns, Republicans cannot be taken for granted after the convention. Moderate surrogates must stomp the Republican circuit and talk to moderate leaders down to the county level in these five states to win their allegiance. It might even make sense to name some cabinet possibilities, which would include prominent moderates, especially George Bush. Great efforts must also be made to tell them about Reagan's attractive record as governor of California. They do not know it now. Perhaps early media budgets could be spent in these states to get the message out.

Without derogating the importance of these two constituencies, they can be won if the RFP organizations in the states are adequately funded, organized, and managed; and if they are vigorously supported by a national RFP top-level surrogates program. The *real* test of the campaign is its ability to attract the BCEC voter. This will win or lose the election. Because of the importance of the BCEC voter in this election, Ronald Reagan himself must be assigned the job of winning this voter over.

Reagan must drive home four issues to do this. *First,* there must be an aggressive supply-side, increase-production economic policy which emphasizes job-creation, tax cuts, and increased future income for all workers. The appeal must not be antiunion; it should criticize Carter's performance using his own "misery index," but it should have a positive thrust.

Second, Reagan must show he will restore America's position in the world as a respected power, without evoking a too-aggressive image. Peace through strength should be the thrust of the appeal. This policy should include a sympathetic understanding of the plight of the nations under Soviet domination in Europe and Asia, including a commitment to broadcasting a message of hope through Radio Free Europe, Radio Liberty, and the Voice of America. There should be an intelligent anticommunist thread oriented around the very serious international disorder created by Carter's incompetence and Soviet ambitions. Ethnics, but also the other BCEC groups, have a deep concern about, family experience with, and attraction toward these issues.

Third, Reagan must stress his accomplishments as governor of California. BCEC voters have some doubts about Reagan's leadership, making comparisons to Carter's lack of experience in Washington. California's size still needs stressing, as does his tax and welfare record. Especially, Reagan should note the competent associates he brought into government, and will bring to Washington. Suggested cabinet-position possibilities for BCEC-background individuals and names of those appointed in California would also be helpful.

Finally, the most difficult political issue of right-to-life must be faced. It is difficult because the antiabortion stance taken by Reagan will cost him 4 percent of the vote. And some of them, for example, liberal Republicans, otherwise would vote for him. Yet our polls also show we can gain up to 8 percent on this issue from prolifers. The campaign must courageously accept the 4 percent loss to obtain the 4 percent net advantage. On the other hand, nothing says the issue must be played excessively or emotionally; rather, reason should be the most characteristic aspect of this appeal.

These issues must be backed by Reagan appearances in ethnic neighborhoods and at important BCEC functions. The Italian Market appearance in Philadelphia, the Polish National Alliance visit in Chicago, and the Ukrainian festival in New Jersey should serve as models. All of this needs support from national RFP and our own state RFP operations. These activities and collateral "Democrats for Reagan" operations are too important to be assigned to the party, with all of its coordination problems between candidates. The states in this region must be backed by sufficient financial resources, beyond their electoral vote weight, and BCEC media appeals should be extensive, especially through the ethnic and Catholic media.

The Reagan Victory Strategy

A Reagan victory is based upon the western and solid Republican states, with the addition of the Frontier South, and the targeting of the Northern Belt, West to East.

All state RFPs should receive adequate organizational budgets, somewhat smaller in the solid Republican states, and somewhat larger in the Northern Belt. Scarce resources such as the candidate's time and media money should be prioritized to the Northern Belt (internally weighted by electoral vote), then the Frontier South, and finally the other two regions. First-rate surrogate programs should be assigned to the Frontier South and to Republican organizations in the Northern Belt. And Reagan himself must lead the targeting appeal.

The key is to reach out to the BCEC voter and switch his allegiance from the New Deal Democratic coalition to the Reagan Republican coalition. There is a trend in this direction already under way. As a matter of course, a successful switch of the BCEC voter will create what we political scientists call a realigning election, which will establish only the seventh new era of American politics. Then the stage is set to fulfill Ronald Reagan's promise to "make America great again."

Chapter 8

The Reagan Victory in 1980*

DAVID BRODER, the widely respected *Washington Post* political reporter, called the 1980 election "the most volatile election campaign in modern times." As readers of this book now know, both the winning electoral coalition strategy and the results actually were predictable at least four years ago.

The proof? As early as 1972, it was clear as I prepared my book on American political culture that the people were still basically conservative after decades of the New Deal. Building on this fact, I offered, a few days after the 1976 general election, a strategy that I was certain would lead to victory in four years: win the Republican nomination for Ronald Reagan, relying on the 20 percent of the electorate that are firmly conservative; after nomination, on the 10 percent of the voting population composed of Republican "middle-of-the-roaders"; and then target social conservatives who have been traditional Democratic voters, for another 20 percent.

I was not alone in this view; syndicated columnist James J. Kilpatrick agreed with my analysis in a column published a few weeks later.

In late December, a few days before Christmas 1976, I sent a letter to all members of the Republican National Committee analyzing the results of an election day exit poll performed by CBS and the *New York Times*. The poll asked whom the person actually voted for, Ford or Carter, and whom that person *would have voted for* had the race been between Reagan and Carter. The results showed Reagan

---

*Based upon a presentation given at the University of Maryland in November 1980 following the election.

even with, or ahead of, Ford in every region. But in the South, Reagan had a 4 percent edge, and that would have been enough to win the election. Ronald Reagan could have beaten Jimmy Carter even before the Georgian had established a record of four years of failure.

The electoral-college strategy which fleshed out the plan outlined four years earlier appeared in the preceding chapter. It was a regional strategy, based upon the western and solid Republican states (New Hampshire, Vermont, Indiana, Oklahoma, and Virginia), with the addition of the Frontier South (Texas, Mississippi, Louisiana, and Florida), and the targeting of the Northern Belt (from Illinois to New Jersey), west to east.

Written at the moment when the nomination was wrapped up, the memo to Casey and Wirthlin stressed the importance of going after that last critical 20 percent of the electorate not usually found in the Republican column: "The key is to reach out to the BCEC (blue-collar, ethnic, Catholic) voter and switch his allegiance from the New Deal coalition to the Reagan Republican coalition. There is a trend in this direction already under way. As a matter of course, a successful switch of the BCEC voter will create what we political scientists call a realigning election, which will establish only the seventh new era of American politics."

Despite much of the media criticism of the Reagan/ Bush campaign leadership, there is ample evidence to show that they did follow a coherent strategy, modified, of course, to accommodate changes in events. Both Casey and campaign chairman Paul Laxalt expressed their approval of my strategy paper shortly after receiving it. It was not until September 19, 1980, that the polls began to show the desired shift among target groups, but the trend was clearly evident after that.

Even the magnitude of the victory was predictable well before the fact, although I must confess that at times I had doubts. I have long believed that the key to predicting elections, both presidential and congressional, is the rating people give on how well the incumbent president performs his job. The *Washington Post* described my belief in an article on January 27, 1974. Application of this performance rating concept allowed a successful prediction of the Republican disaster in the congressional elections later that year.

I took the opportunity to apply this formula again well before the 1980 success to predict: "If he can sustain majority approval, Carter can be reelected. If not, and this is more probable, the Republicans can be predicted to win the presidential election in 1980." When the formula is applied to the 1980 election, it predicts a Carter vote of 43 percent, compared with the actual 42 percent. Even the 37 percent predicted nine months before the election was reasonably close to the actual results.

This formulation was useful in the decision-making process in the campaign. As deputy director of political planning and analysis of the Reagan/Bush campaign, I relied upon it to provide advice on whether Ronald Reagan should agree to debate President Carter. I advised political director Bill Timmons that Governor Reagan should debate.

Using presidential job performance as a controlling factor, I analyzed the undecided vote and concluded that Reagan had enough advantage to win the election. Yet, it appeared to me that our support was soft at that point, with a core of only 30.8 percent. It was clear that we could not sustain two weeks of media criticism that Ronald Reagan was afraid of Jimmy Carter.

My reasoning went this way: "I marginally lean toward doing it [the debate]. I just cannot believe that he [Reagan] would fumble it; he is a master of this format. In addition, Carter's momentum—if he has any—is slowed up, as people await the outcome of the debate. The most likely outcome is a draw between the candidates. That draw ensures us the election."

Political science gets some rough treatment at the hands

both of practical politicians and of the media. A common view is that it is like the Holy Roman Empire: it neither is political nor does it have any scientific laws.

Political science is not an exact science. But it can produce theories that have great value. Sir Ernest Barker's— that the voter's general evaluation of government performance is how the ordinary citizen makes his influence felt— was a good guide in 1980, as it has been since 1944, as shown in the Appendix. And the concept of political culture posits that these perceptions rest upon a stable set of values. A political scientist relying upon this theory could predict the 1980 election well before November 4. That's not bad for a science so dependent on the assumption that voters in elections are not volatile.

Predictions for the future can be based upon the same reasoning. The key facts are these: the American people retain their belief in their conservative values; but this belief is still only inchoate, and can be affected by events, media distortion, and attacks from opposing politicians. That is, the Reagan revolution has momentum, but its success is not ensured.

The Reagan administration must succeed in its policies if it is to be perceived as performing effectively. Following polls that measure popular evaluation of presidential performance will still be the key to predicting future electoral success. This does *not* mean that the president must be perceived as successful at each and every moment during his incumbency. In the short run, difficult decisions can be made at the risk of a momentary drop in performance ratings and, in fact, for the good of the country, must be made.

Over the long haul, however, the president must be perceived to be performing well. The success of the Republican party in the congressional elections of 1982 will depend on it. More important, the future of the Reagan realignment of American politics will depend on it in 1984. If he succeeds, a new entry will be made on the very short list of American electoral eras. His conservative policies will then shape the future generation, and bring the "new beginning" he promised during the campaign.

Chapter 9

The Reagan Coalition: Where Has It Gone?*

A *NEWSWEEK* poll in January 1983 found just 38 percent of those polled thinking President Reagan was doing a good job—compared with 48 percent six months before, and 60 percent in 1981. Gallup found the rating to be 41 percent, and Reagan trailing all recent presidents after two years in office. Lou Harris found 55 percent versus 27 percent believing President Reagan's economic initiatives have failed. In mock election matchups, Gallup found John Glenn (the Democrat's answer to Sominex) leading President Reagan 54 to 39 percent, and Walter Mondale (Chappaquiddick's replacement) leading 52 to 40 percent. Clearly, things are less than perfect for the coalition that elected Ronald Reagan president in 1980.

The Republicans lost twenty-six seats in the House of Representatives and maintained their advantage in the Senate in the 1982 elections. With a 10.1 percent unemployment, the normal out-party edge, Democratic reapportionment gains, a record number of bankruptcies, and poor farm conditions, the Republicans should have lost forty-five seats in the House of Representatives. The political science models make it very clear we won about twenty seats more than we should have won.

The main reason the GOP did so well is that the Democrats did not go on the offensive. As Democratic pollster Pat Caddell said, "The Democrats pulled their punches." Republicans were also better funded, and that

---

* This paper was presented to the American Conservative Political Action Conference in Washington, D.C., on February 17, 1983.

helped too. The Republicans launched their campaign theme—"the Democrats got us into this mess, we have turned inflation around, and we're going to solve unemployment next"—too late; but once adopted, they used it very successfully to limit their losses.

The polls show clearly that *the economy was the issue,* vastly overwhelming all others. Turnout was large because people wanted to send a message that they thought unemployment was too high. This issue made it impossible for the Reagan coalition to form in 1982.

The essential fact in American presidential politics, usually ignored by the media, is that it is based on the electoral-college system: states, not congressional districts or a national majority, count. As I have argued before, there are four fundamental geographical elements in the Reagan electoral coalition.

First, the West, consisting of sixteen states and 126 electoral votes. The West is strong conservative and Republican territory, with a culture of individualism and enterprise which is congruent with the values held by the president. The *second* base area is created from the solid Republican states of New Hampshire, Vermont, Indiana, Oklahoma, and Virginia. These thirty-nine electoral votes also represent areas whose values are compatible with the essential message of Ronald Reagan. The *third* element is to add the South, especially the Frontier South region, consisting of Texas, Mississippi, Louisiana, and Florida (sixty-seven votes). These states have many values and characteristics similar to the two other areas, and although they have been closely contested, the Republicans usually win.

This is a base electoral vote of 232, leaving only thirty-six for victory. To this base must be added the Northern Belt region, running from Illinois to Ohio, to Pennsylvania, and New Jersey. These states represent eighty-eight electoral votes, less than half of which must be won. These belt states are similar in that they have strong Republican bases, but not enough traditional Republicans to win. To this base must be added the traditionally Democratic blue-collar, ethnic, and Catholic (BCEC) voter who shifted to Ronald Reagan in 1980.

Republicans did not receive a majority of the vote among any of the coalition elements, except conservatives and Republicans, in 1982. Republicans did proportionally better among westerners and midwesterners, college-educated, upper-income, and professional-status individuals, as well as among Protestants—although the difference between Protestants and Catholics has narrowed greatly, to only two percent—but they did not win majorities in these groups.

The major new phenomenon in the election was the development of the "marriage gap." It is much larger than the much reported "gender gap." Whereas 49 percent of married men supported Republican candidates, only thirty-seven percent of single men did. Likewise, 44 percent of married women supported Republican candidates, compared to 34 percent of single women. The most disturbing group for Republicans, in fact, was single young men, not women at all. Although the eighteen- to twenty-nine-year-old male voters still tended to call themselves disproportionately Republican, and were more approving of President Reagan than any other group, 62 percent still voted for Democratic House candidates. Support among blue-collar and ethnic voters was similarly weak, indeed, even lower. Again, unemployment—especially among the young—was the most important reason for the lower level of support.

Ronald Reagan survived the election in relatively good shape. The president received his highest recent approval rating, 48 percent approving against 52 disapproving, in the exit polls on election day. Obviously, this must be raised to win in 1984, but it was reasonably good for that time. The president also defeated Mr. Mondale by 47 to 41 percent. Since this was a poll of people who actually vote, this is significant—even though the later polls suggest that this level of approval might have deteriorated since then.

Once the media decided to hype the unemployment statistics, while incorrectly saying the administration cut the safety net, the electoral environment became polluted. Their claim that we have cut most programs to the poor could not be further from the truth. We could have sold our counter message *earlier,* but the media's relentless broadcasting of their message made our task very difficult.

The underlying problem was that Congress did not allow us to pass enough of our program quickly enough so we could get the economy moving. A half century of economic irrationality cannot be solved overnight by half measures. We were not allowed to cut back expenditures nearly as much as we wished, and in fact, government expenses have *grown* as a percentage of gross national product during our administration. Congress spread the tax cuts out over too long a period, at too low a rate. Indeed, Congress has frustrated us at nearly every turn.

We have not been able to make all the *changes* we wanted. But we have shifted the debate; we:

- Reduced nondefense government employment by 100,000.
- Reduced taxes $335 billion through 1985 under Carter projections.
- Reduced the growth rate of domestic spending.
- Increased defense spending to restore America's role in the world.
- Achieved some policy control over government operations.
- Appointed many conservative judges.
- Cut inflation by two thirds.
- Cut interest rates by half.
- Indexed tax rates.

Where Are We Today?

1.   *Policy.* The president made the freeze on the federal government spending, and the structural reform of entitlements, the centerpiece of his State of the Union message. This is good government and good politics. It is a sound theme upon which to work now with the Democrats in Congress, if possible; but also to take to the voters in the future if the Democrats refuse to cooperate. Many fundamental reforms are included in the president's package; these will have excellent long-term, as well as short-term, effects. It is a basically conservative program that will appeal to the Republican and economic-conservative base vote, which is necessary for electoral success in 1984.

The president's program will also put the nation on the road to recovery, and to solving the problem of unemployment. Because of congressional inaction, recovery was delayed. But the essential steps have been taken, and the economy is correcting. When it hits full stride, as it will in the next few months, a permanent basis for growth will be set. This program will put us in an excellent position before the election in 1984, to appeal to presently disaffected voters—especially single young men—to get them back into the coalition.

It is significant that the president renewed his commitments on social issues too. "God should never have been expelled from the classroom," he noted as he pledged his support for a constitutional amendment to permit voluntary school prayer. Likewise, the president renewed his endorsement for tuition tax credits, and his opposition to abortion on demand. Each of these issues appeals to that BCEC voter so critical to the coalition's success in 1984. Indeed, the president's commitment to a strong defense helps with this group too.

2.   *Candidate.* My personal impression is that Ronald Reagan will run for reelection. Of course, he has not said he

will, but that is my view. As shown by the polls taken on election day, the president is strong, but his degree of electoral support must be increased. And that is where we need you, the activists who began Ronald Reagan's quest for the presidency. As the economy improves, our task should be made easier; and it looks promising. With the rise in factory orders by a record 12 percent in December 1982, a private economist, Michael K. Evans, who has been among the less optimistic analysts, said: "I think the recession is over. The pessimists are being left in the dust." But to win, we need your support.

A detailed *New York Times*/CBS News poll taken in January 1983 shows the president's essential strengths. After two years of making tougher decisions than any other recent president, 41 percent of the public still said that they approve of the way he is handling his job, compared to 42 percent for a relatively inactive President Carter in 1979. His approval for foreign policy was 39 percent versus Carter's 34 percent, and for economic policy 35 percent versus Carter's 28 percent. So, relatively, there is a base that has remained firm notwithstanding two difficult years of readjusting a half century of liberal failure.

The most hopeful fact is that perceptions of Ronald Reagan remain positive, so that the basic vote can be expanded: 53 percent still believe Ronald Reagan is a strong leader, 52 percent are optimistic about the next two years under his presidency, 60 percent believe he is a competent person, and 60 percent believe he offers a vision of where he wants to move the country.

The president has offered the olive leaf of bipartisanship, but the Democratic Congress has already flatly rejected it. Although the administration is still committed to making bipartisanship work, I must admit that I am pessimistic. The fact is, *we need another election.*

Congressional elections do not give as complete a reading of the public as does a presidential election, and are often inconclusive, as was this past election. Congress needs another presidential election for it to get a true reading of the popular mood. We need an election, staffed by you, the people who got us here, so that you can take the president's real message to the people. I myself look forward to the coming campaign so that the president can take his conservative program to the voters. When he does, I have no doubt that there will be a broad movement by all elements of the coalition to the president.

The resulting broad approval generated by the 1984 election will guarantee the success of the full Reagan agenda in the second Reagan administration. The president and his coalition will have then permanently set the foundation for restoring America's greatness.

Chapter 10

A Strategy for 1984

TO: JAMESON G. Campaigne, Jr., Secretary, American Conservative Union.
From: Dr. Donald J. Devine.
Subject: 1984 Election Strategy.

You have asked me to share my thoughts with the ACU board regarding the issues that I think will be important in the next election, before we get into that contest. In my view, five issue areas dominate presidential elections: the economy, foreign policy, control of spending, social issues, and governing. The economy has dominated the issue arena so far, and will continue to be the preeminent issue, but it is also important for the next election to give attention to the others.

1. *The Economy.* As the administration has solved the inflation problem, the general public has shifted its attention to unemployment. There is a clear "what have you done for me lately" attitude of the population at large. Whereas inflation used to be mentioned as the most important problem, unemployment is now mentioned by a three-to-one ratio (54 to 18 percent in April 1983). At the end of February, only 33 percent gave the president excellent or good ratings for his handling of the economy (up 4 percent from the month before), and a similar one third gave the president credit for getting the country out of the recession. On the other hand, March polls showed that a majority of 54 percent said that the president was trying to reduce unemployment, and 67 percent said that he was making a real effort to repair the economy.

The critical fact is that only 42 percent believe the recession is over, compared to 53 percent who do not. This is the theme we will have to stress with the general voter: that the recession is over and that President Reagan is the one responsible for achieving this recovery. We must point out how well we have done on inflation, interest rates, and the other economic indicators to prove the recession is over. We should ask whether the voters want to roll back this progress by voting Democratic, or whether they want the recovery to continue under the president.

2. *Foreign Policy.* The April 1983 Gallup poll showed that 11 percent of people (the third highest percentage) thought the danger of war was the greatest problem facing America. Fortunately, the March ABC News/*Washington Post* poll found that 61 percent believed the president would not lead us into a war. Likewise, 60 percent found him a strong leader. On "handling foreign policy," however, only 37 percent gave an excellent or pretty good rating, compared to 59 percent that rated him fair or poor. Only 32 percent supported the handling of the situation in the Middle East. Therefore, there is a basic sense of trust for the president on foreign policy, but concern for specific issues. Foreign policy rarely dominates national elections, but it will be necessary to cite the facts and create the symbols (e.g., trips abroad) that build the president's image as a strong and responsible world leader.

3. *Controlling Government Spending.* This issue is clearly one of the president's strongest points, appealing to his basically conservative and Republican constituency. But most do not believe he has done enough: 54 percent say he has done too little to cut the size of the federal government, and 54 percent say he has done too little to get the federal government to live within its means. Here is clear proof that there is a conservative majority for cutting the size of government, and even that we should do more in this direction. While the conservative middle class believes the

president has not done enough to cut the costs of government, 62 percent also believe he has been unfair to the poor. It is critical that we emphasize what the president has done in attempting to keep government spending down, while maintaining the safety net, in the face of a Congress that is irresponsible in its spending habits.

4. *Social Issues.* Social issues are the most divisive to the basic coalition, especially for liberal Republicans. As we have found over the past two years, the social issues cannot be avoided and must be embraced enthusiastically or there will be negative fallout, with little positive effect. The basic theme of "God, family, work, freedom, democracy, and country" (raised recently in the San Antonio speech) still has extremely wide support among the American people. It is this basic theme that allows the president to reach most broadly into the populace as a whole, and appeal to the fundamental American culture. It is also an area where the population is closely divided over specific issues, which appeal to blue-collar ethnic Catholics, Hispanics, and traditional and southern Protestants—issues like abortion, quotas, school prayer, tuition tax credits, education, crime, welfare rules, and so forth. Social issues basically are a strong theme for the president, but one in which specific issues have to be communicated adroitly.

5. *Governing.* The governing issue reaches beyond the basic coalition to independent voters, while also being in accord with the opinions of the basic constituency. Federalism, regulatory reform, private sector initiatives, making government more effective (the Reform 88 project), and the civil-service reform themes already begun are examples. In the ABC News March 1983 poll, 55 percent said that the president was cutting waste in government. The election of Jimmy Carter in 1976 proved that reforming the bureaucracy also is good politics and good government: a Wirthlin poll found that 27 percent of people thought that Ronald Reagan had cut the number of federal employees enough,

and 46 percent thought he had not cut enough, compared to only 17 percent that thought employment was cut too much. When asked, regarding reducing the number of government employees, who should keep their jobs—those who do the best job or those with the most seniority—69 percent strongly agreed and an additional 16 percent agreed somewhat that retention should be based upon performance.

The Congress may present us with an issue here by blocking our civil-service reforms, so we can truly say "they will not let us govern effectively." We can be in Washington and against it. The fact of the matter is, the Reagan administration has run the government well, within the limits Congress has let us do so. We should make that fact known. We also have reduced the number of nondefense employees by 113,000 since we entered office, the largest amount since World War II. The "governing" issue is a positive one which can help sell the accomplishments of this administration.

Approval of Presidential Performance. Approval ratings for President Reagan by the general population have gone through three stages. First, from the 1980 election until June 1981 over 67 percent supported the president. Second, from September 1981 until February 1982 a clear majority supported the president. Yet, for a long third period—from March 1982 until March 1983—the president was supported by only his base constituency, about 40 percent of the population. It is important that the president was able to maintain this base of support through that difficult period of his presidency. He made tough decisions and his base vote stuck with him. Moreover, it is becoming clearer that the low point of approval was at the end of January 1983. By February, it had gone from a 35 percent low back to 40 percent. Interestingly, support for the Republican party went down in that period—suggesting that Senate attempts to separate themselves from the president will not work for the Republicans. One recent poll even suggests that, by

April, the president had come out of the third period and entered a fourth period of majority support.

I will throw in a *prediction* for free. If we run a well-organized campaign and sell the issues as suggested here, I predict that we will win as broad an election victory in 1984 as we did in 1980. We start out in a good position on the issues—the people basically are conservative, and they are beginning to recognize our accomplishments. With presidential approval at about 50 percent, which now appears likely, my model of presidential elections predicts that the president will win a resounding victory. I also feel it in my bones. But we must organize effectively if that potential is to be realized.

Appendix

Predicting the 1980 Election*

A COMMON complaint is that political scientists have no scientific laws. It is in the field of voting and survey research that the presumed lack of a predictive law is most embarrassing. After all, the major investment of talent and resources in the modern era of political science has been made in this arena of study. Moreover, voting is both relatively easy to study and important for democracy, while polling accuracy was used as early proof that politics could be scientific.

At one time, the taunt of no scientific laws was deflected by a reference to the theory of the normal vote, and an emphasis upon the powerful explainer, party identification. Recent research and analysis in political science, however, now make that claim somewhat questionable. First, party identification is assumed by the theory to be stable, or relatively stable. If it is stable, however, it is not a true predictor. It has more the status of a constant in a scientific equation, since true predictors vary. Therefore, the variables of "issues" and "candidates" must be entered into the theory to predict which party will win, given these particular circumstances. These are so diverse, multiple, and idiosyncratic, however, that issues and candidate qualities hardly fit the category of lawlike predictors. Second, much research now questions whether party identification is stable. In that case, there is no "normal" for the vote, and the logic of the whole theory is questionable. Third, some

---

*Written in January 1979, this article is included here because it is referred to many times in the main text. It is the basic political science model upon which predicting electoral success in democracies rests.

evidence suggests that party overlaps with issues and candidate perception, making party identification a less important explainer of voting. Finally, party identification has been found to hide several subsidiary elements, making the concept itself subject to question.

Today, 70 percent of the population does not identify strongly with a political party. Those not identifying with a party at all, or Independents, especially have been increasing over time: doubling, in fact, from 16 percent of the population in 1937 to 33 percent in 1976. In addition, party is by no means transferred to all children even where there is a party transfer. By the 1970s there were almost as many Democratic and Republican parents who did not have children of the same party as did. Finally, although the gross totals of party identifiers did not change much in the 1950s and 1960s, there have been major shifts between the party categories which have canceled each other. It appears that at least one fifth of the electorate has changed party identification in these canceling shifts. During the sixteen years between 1952 and 1968, young northern whites shifted 13 percentage points from Democratic to Independent. The shift of young southern whites was even stronger: from 62 percent Democratic in 1952 to only 26 percent Democratic in 1968. Blacks increased their Democratic identification 30 percentage points, from 53 to 83 percent. Analysis of shifts to Independent identification shows an 18 percent shift among Catholics away from Democratic and an 11 percent change among college-educated away from Republican identification.

Either party identification is the principal explanatory factor in voting or it is not. If it is not—that is, if party overlaps significantly and logically with issues and candidate perception—the whole theory of normal vote is questionable. If party identification is the chief explanatory factor, it may be relatively stable or unstable. If it is stable, party basically is a constant rather than a lawlike predictor. If it is not stable, again, the whole theory comes into question.

The Theory of Authority Evaluation

There is an alternative theory in political science, however, which does not have these difficulties. The theory simply holds that how the public evaluates the performance of the political authority in office will determine who will be the next such officeholder. If the voters believe the incumbent has done well, they will reelect him or vote for his party. If they think he has done poorly, they will vote against him or his party.

The authority-evaluation theory is most compatible with democratic theory. It holds that the evaluation made by the people of authority performance will determine who will rule. It creates a nice responsibility between party performance (or rather perceived performance) and future rule of that party. Indeed, before the empirical findings, Sir Ernest Barker had theorized that evaluation of overall authority performance, rather than issue or ideological voting, was a more reasonable means for popular control of government. And empirical research, beginning with that of V. O. Key, Jr., has substantiated that there is a relationship.

It is now possible to look at this relationship in a more systematic manner. For the 1968, 1972, and 1976 elections, the Survey Research Center/Center for Political Studies at the University of Michigan asked those in its sample to evaluate presidential performance before the election, and then compared this with their reported vote after the election. Table 24 reports the correlations for those years. But the percentages alone show the pattern: in 1968, 80 percent of those who thought Johnson did very well as

Table 24
Relationship Between Authority Evaluation and Vote

Question: In general, how do you feel about how President Johnson has done his job? Would you rate his handling of American problems over the past four years as very good, good, fair, poor, or very poor?

A. Evaluation of Democratic President Performance, 1968

Reported vote, 1968	Very Good	Good	Fair	Poor	Very Poor
Vote for Democrat	80%	58%	35%	11%	4%
Vote against Democrat	20	42	65	89	96

d = .337   pv. < .001

Question: Do you approve or disapprove of the way Nixon is handling his job as president?

B. Evaluation of Republican President Performance, 1972

Reported vote, 1972	Approve	Neutral	Disapprove
Vote for Republican	83%	51%	14%
Vote against Republican	17	49	86

d = .596   pv. < 001

Question: Do you approve or disapprove of the way Ford is handling his job as president?

C. Evaluation of Republican President Performance, 1976

Reported vote, 1976	Approve	Neutral	Disapprove
Vote for Republican	74%	39%	9%
Vote against Republican	26	61	91

d = .569   pv < .001

SOURCE: Center for Political Studies, University of Michigan, Election Studies from the Inter-University Consortium for Political Research.

---

president voted for the Democrat, Humphrey, whereas 96 percent of those who thought performance very poor voted against him. Likewise, in 1972, 83 percent who approved Nixon's performance voted for him, and 86 percent who disapproved voted against him. Again, in 1976, 74 percent of those who approved of Ford's performance voted for him, and 91 percent who disapproved voted for the Democrat, Carter.

In all three elections, the percentages run strongly and monotonously across the degrees of the evaluation. But it is clear that a poor evaluation of performance hurts a president more than a positive one helps. Whereas 70 to 80 percent vote for a president if they approve his performance, 85 to 95 percent vote against a president or his party if they disapprove. This is in accord with other literature which emphasizes the importance of "negative" voting.

The importance of this authority-evaluation variable can be shown by comparing its explanatory power to that of the other major factors in influencing the vote. Table 25, therefore, reports the most important predictors I have found in explaining the vote using the SRC/CPS data base. Evaluation of presidential performance is among the most powerful. Of the social background variables, only race compares favorably with it; but the evaluation variable is stronger in two of the three available years. Ideology and opinion on issues sometimes explain rather well, but not to the degree that evaluation does.

In two of the three available comparisons of Table 25, evaluation of presidential performance was a more powerful explainer than party identification. This is the relevant comparison. Even the exception, in 1968, is clouded by the greater number of evaluation categories and by including Nixon and Wallace under: "Vote against the Democratic" incumbent. This correlation remains after it is controlled for party identification. Yet, party also holds when authority evaluation is controlled. The best conclusion is that both presidential evaluation and party identification independently explain when the other is controlled. Yet, the relative power of the evaluation variable is impressive. And, theoretically, it can be used alone as a varying predictor, that is, one which is actually related to the performance of government.

The compatibility of a highly predictive authority-

Table 25
Correlations Between Most Explanatory Variables and Vote[1]

	1952	1956	1960	1964	1968	1972	1976
Party identification	.502	.514	.540	.385	.418	.322	.416
Evaluation of pres. pref.	NA	NA	NA	NA	.337	.596	.569
Domestic political ideology[2]	.249	NA	NA	.351	.261	NS	NS
Race	.412	.269	.238	.345	.607	.540	.478
Class (income)	.076	NS	NS	.085	NS	.080	.140
Opinion on central gov't aid to education	NA	.098	.209	.233	.261	NA	NA
Opinion on gov't medical care	NA	.202	.196	.333	.261	.114	.246
Opinion on central gov't Negro job guarantee	.125	NS	NS	.196	.210	.209	NA
Opinion on school integration	NA	NS	NS	.161	.231	.230	.116
Opinion on military spending	NA	NA	NA	NA	NA	.317	.188
Opinion on inflation	NA	NA	NA	NA	NA	NA	.349

SOURCE: CPS, University of Michigan.

[1]All correlations are d. All are pv. < 001 except NS, based upon S.
[2]Operationalized by "Government in Washington Is Getting Too Powerful." The correlation using subjective ideology, however, was .319 in 1972 and .369 in 1976.

evaluation variable with democratic theory is highlighted by another control. SRC/CPS analysts say that levels of political sophistication are critical factors for a realistic test of democratic voting. Democratic theory expects the less sophisticated to be able to make relevant voting evaluations about as well as do the sophisticated. Rather than the crude index of years of schooling, though, the more theoretically meaningful attentiveness variable will be used here. This control shows that those more attentive to politics translated their evaluation into a vote quite well in 1968, 1972, and 1976. In those years, almost no attentive who thought the president performed poorly voted for that authority's party (and the few who did may merely have thought the other party's candidate would do worse). On the other hand, the nonattentive were just as rational in their evaluation, since the relationship was only slightly lower in 1968 and was even slightly higher in 1972 than was that for the more attentive. That is, as expected by democratic theory, evaluation of authorities is not affected by levels of sophistication among the electorate.

Conclusion

A political science law can help predict elections. Other variables can partially explain how individuals will vote. Yet, evaluation of presidential performance alone consistently has been a powerful predictor. It is not assumed to be stable, and therefore it truly is a predictor. It is an evaluation of performance which changes over time. But it is not as idiosyncratic and diverse as issue or unique candidate factors. Evaluation is made of a single, constant object—the authority in question, here the president.

The findings are unambiguous. If the people like the president's performance, they will vote for him or his party. If they do not, they will vote against him or his party. Although a belief that the president is performing well does not help the president as much as a belief that he is performing poorly will hurt, the president has received at least a three-to-one ratio of support from those who approve of his performance. If they disapprove of his performance, almost nine in ten have voted against the president.

Although there are only a few data points across time, one may even put the relationship in a more lawlike form. Figure 1 shows the linear relationship between the percentage of presidential approval measured in the last months in which data were available before the elections, and the percent of the vote obtained by the president's party in the elections, from 1940 to 1976.

Figure 1.   Relationship Between Presidential Approval in Last Month Measured Before the Election and Vote for Incumbent's Party, 1940–76

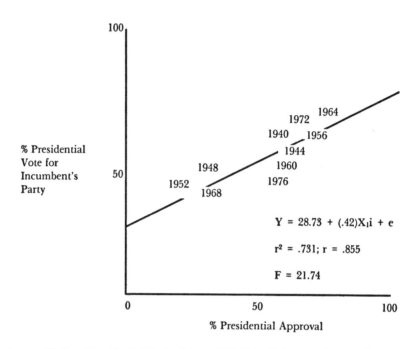

SOURCE: Hadley Cantril, *Public Opinion, 1935–1946* (Princeton, N.J.: Princeton University Press, 1951), p. 756; "Presidential Popularity," *Gallup Opinion Index* (February 1970), pp. 8–15; CPS (1972 and 1976), *Election Studies*, ICPR.

The r^2 of .731 shows extremely good fit for the line. The linear regression law is: % vote = 28.73% + (.42) % approval + e. A president, therefore, "starts" with about 29 percent of the vote. For every 1 percent increase in approval, a president can expect 0.4 percent increase in his party's vote in the next election. If the election were held a year before its actual date, for example, Jimmy Carter could be estimated to receive about 37 percent of the vote. A president or his party would need about 51 percent approval to receive a majority vote in the election.

The authority-evaluation law allows us to make predictions. Almost a year before the fact, evaluations can change. As a result of the Iran crisis, Carter's evaluation has increased dramatically. Yet, it seems likely that when that event fades, Carter's evaluation will also. Past evidence suggests Jimmy Carter will not be reelected president in 1980. According to the law, no other Democrat should be able to be elected either. Of course, as with any probabilistic law, there may be anomalies, and Iran and the mystique of Edward Kennedy may be such. If one must predict, however, it makes more sense to use the law of authority evaluation even this far before the election.

In any event, the reader can follow the popular evaluations of Carter's performance. If he can sustain majority approval, Carter can be reelected. If not, and this is more probable, the Republicans can be predicted to win the presidential election in 1980. That is a political science law.